RE-PURPOSE YOURSELF

How to Get Hired After 50

Alex J. Bodnar

10-10-10
Publishing

RE-PURPOSE YOURSELF
www.turning50today.com

Limits of Liability and Disclaimer of Warranty
The author and publisher shall not be liable for your misuse of the enclosed material. This book is strictly for informational and educational purposes only.

Warning – Disclaimer
The purpose of this book is to educate and entertain. The author and/or publisher do not guarantee that anyone following these techniques, suggestions, tips, ideas, or strategies will become successful. The author and/or publisher shall have neither liability nor responsibility to anyone with respect to any loss or damage caused, or alleged to be caused, directly or indirectly by the information contained in this book.

Medical Disclaimer
The medical or health information in this book is provided as an information resource only and is not to be used or relied on for any diagnostic or treatment purposes. This information is not intended to be patient education, does not create any patient-physician relationship, and should not be used as a substitute for professional diagnosis and treatment.

Publisher
First 10-10-10 Publishing paperback edition October 2019
Markham, ON Canada

Printed in Canada and the United States of America

Contents

I dedicate this book to my late father, Frank, who was and always will be my hero. His love for his family, his ambition, and his determination to re-purpose himself as he grew older is my inspiration for this book, and the fuel for my journey.

Dad, you are my guardian angel!

Foreword

The corporate culture accommodates the expense of severance packages as the cost of doing business. However, you are more than the weeks of compensation that you are allocated on a budget line after dedicating your time, energy and focus to climbing the corporate ladder. One day, you are pushed off that ladder and left hanging, wondering how to grab hold of your self-respect, self-worth and self-esteem.

In *Re-Purpose Yourself*, author Alex Bodnar provides you with his story of depression, shame and addiction, which he experienced as he learned to accept that he is worth more to the world than a budget line expense. He shows you that you can make your life goals a reality by envisioning your second act in life, by learning from his research, his intelligence and his resilience as he faced his fear of failure and insecurities. The average life expectancy continues to rise, and is now reported to be 81 years of age for men and women. This book will show you that you can work the way you want, and live a fulfilled life when you are faced with ageism during career transition and job loss.

I had the pleasure to witness the great insights that Alex offered while participating in my personal development seminars. His candor and inquisitive nature inspire you to think differently about accomplishing your goals and realizing the ultimate power in your thoughts and dreams. His passion for life will ignite your belief that anything is possible. His self-reflections and observations provide you with great insights into the resilience of the human spirit. His personal search for his re-purposed life serves as a great guide as you define your next chapter in your book called Life. This book provides you with examples from his journey, and stories from others, so you can recognize the challenges facing job loss and career transition. You take a seat on his emotional roller coaster as he describes the ups and downs of managing his fears of ageism, addiction and shame. This book will help you to be stronger, wiser and smarter, and re-purpose yourself during career transition.

Raymond Aaron
New York Times Bestselling Author

Acknowledgements

I thank my husband, **Sean MacKinnon**, who has been my champion, my best friend, and my soul mate. He stands by me as I experience tremendous surges of success and shocking blows of failure. His optimism, love, and respect has always been essential for my mental health and well-being that continues to grow our relationship, which is God's most precious gift in my life.

Secondly, I thank my family who have been my foundation for the many joys that I celebrate with them every year at Christmas, birthdays, and anytime we get together. My eternal gratitude to my mother, **Christine Bodnar**, who has always given more than she receives. Thanks to my brother, **Frank Bodnar**, for showing me what dedication to the family truly means. Thank you to my sister, **Natalia Bodnar**, for showing me what transformation can look like. Thank you to my niece, **Kyara Vizcaino**, who has more talent and intelligence than anyone I know. Thanks to my extended family: **Anna Yeandle, Jeff Yeandle, Mary Wegiel, John Wegiel, Mandy Van Egdom, Adam Van Egdom, Justin Wegiel, Debbie Fishwick, Jeremy Yeandle, Karisha Yeandle** and **Katie Yeandle,** who have been my cheerleaders who believe in me when I doubt myself.

I am grateful for my amazing, supportive in-laws, who have shown me the value of love and respect like any *normal* family. Thank you to **Lisa Arseneau, Denis Arseneau, Leslie Guerette, Fernand Guerette, Céline Sundquist, Max Sundquist, Philip Arseneau, Christopher Guerette, Melissa Guerette, Beverly Cornwall, Rob Cornwall,** and my father in law, **Philip MacKinnon**, and his partner, **Beverley Marchuk**.

I am blessed to have some brilliant people who continue to exceed my expectations in making my life goal a reality as we grow our theatre company together. **Paul Louie**, who has continued to show his selflessness, as he values community to bring joy and success to those who want to grow their talents and skills. To my amazing theatre management team, who have been instrumental in working to build quality into every production: **Nicole Bailey, Helen Conway, Carole Mills, Randy Bridge, Heather Bridge, Maria Michelli** and **Ren Howard**. Also, thank you to the extraordinary people who have inspired me to envision the creation of a professional theatre company within our community: **Sarah Rice, Kirsten Souwand, Dan Souwand,** and **Corwin Howard**. All these individuals give more than they are asked, to share my vision of my re-purposed life.

Lastly, I thank three special women who have been there for me for as long as I can remember. **Kaylie McCann, Paula Midena**, and **Thérèse Anne Sidler** have listened to my dreams and fed my heart with joy and peace when I needed it most.

I thank you for allowing me to share my thoughts and vulnerable moments of my life for you to interpret how to meet challenges when you get kicked out of your tribe. I have experienced great healing from speaking about my depression and determination to find ways to use my talents to help others as I have always done as my authentic life purpose. I am grateful to you for learning from my story, to re-purpose your skills and talents after years of working for someone else who no longer needs or cares about you.

Chapter 1: Know Thyself

"It's true in everything, not just in drag: To be a success, you have to understand the landscape. You have to know thyself, and you have to know your history so that you can draw from people who have figured out the equation you are faced with. It's not rocket science."
– RuPaul

1

I am now 53 years old. After working for over twenty years at two of Canada's largest insurance companies, I find myself out of work for the third time over the last 5 years. WOW!

Now I wonder why. Why is this happening to me? Why is this happening again? What am I doing right?

What am I doing wrong? What should I be doing? What didn't I do to stay employed?

What will happen to me if I never find another job?

All these tough questions are swirling around in my head and consuming my thoughts. This is really happening to me, and more importantly, it's probably happening to you.

When it's happening, all I can do is wonder how I am going to find the next opportunity that fits my skills, my experience, my passion, and my life. Oh, right, these are my wonder years. That is what I am calling this period in my life. Welcome to the wonder years! I'm on a journey over the next year, and I must find myself. I didn't know I was lost until I felt lost. This is self-awareness. What a concept.

I think to myself that I am self-aware. I know I have strong leadership skills, and I know I communicate well because I can lead service professionals in business. I know that I can train and facilitate meetings because that's how I've performed at work most of my life. I've learnt how to be in control even when everything around me appears to be out of control. Now what do I do? I panic.

I put on my professional businessman face to manage my panic. What else can I do? I act like I am still working despite what's happened to me. I go to work by attending networking sessions that I arrange, and I attend workshops focused on the job of finding a job. I research the best way to use tools like LinkedIn, search engines, recruiter sites, target company job boards, job market reports, social media sites sharing company insights, and the list goes on.

Here's how it goes... I find myself going through the motions of connecting with people. I am connecting with people that I've never met before and yet rely on now for my self-worth. That's a scary situation because most people who know you, know you for two reasons: First, the social perspective of seeing how you interact with others, how and when you listen to others, how you respond to others, how you co-ordinate your efforts with others, how you keep your promises, and more importantly, what they think of you; and second, it's how people look to you to be a respected and productive contributor in society, and not pose a risk to them. So, what does it mean to be a respected and productive contributor in society?

I have been going through a lot of personal discoveries, and I've realized that the way you contribute to society is the way you take care of yourself. If you can't take care of yourself, then you really can't contribute to society. That is the simple truth. I am at a point in my life where I have done a lot of personality tests, such as Myers Briggs Type Indicator, what color is my rainbow, what colour is my parachute, etc. I think most of the results represented who I wanted others to see me as, because a couple of identifiers were true: a caring, emotionally-driven visionary who can see things and describe future states of being for other people, who may not at the time. This idea of being self-aware has always been somewhat of a misnomer to me, because my self-awareness happens when I react to stimuli based on my self-imposed pressures and fears. I get excited by the energy that is coming at me, which is typical of my extraversion.

I go to my first coaching session with my career transition coach because I've been through this before. The two insurance companies that have released me are paying for a transition company to ease the anxiety of being unwanted. After two minutes of detailing my experiences, and outlining my desire to stay engaged with others, and my drive to avoid the feelings of being broken, she can see that I am in an anxious state, riddled with frustration, deliberation, and expectation, all rolled up into an *open and transparent* person. She says to me that I am self-aware, and I think to myself, *what does that mean?* What does it mean to be self-aware? As everyone knows, during a job search, you must know who you are, what skills you have, what you like to do, what you don't like to do, what motivates you in the morning, and what doesn't motivate you in the morning. All these considerations are needed so that I can script my 90-second elevator speech. I am seducing others, using my best storytelling abilities to seek a champion for me in their circles of influence. The adage of *"it's not what you know; it's who you know,"* suddenly becomes my self-awareness.

Here I am, trying to control my responses to the stimuli coming at me, and for some reason, I can't seem to control my responses. My *normal* self in a work environment is a professional that seeks to understand and wants to be understood: someone that focuses on the priorities of the day and the long-term impacts, who seeks to improve working conditions and ease of business; someone that can schedule himself and encourage others to come along for the ride. Now I can't control myself from the time I wake up, because I have the feeling of being in a constant struggle with myself, and I'm feeling frustrated because I lack energy, I like focus, and I lack concentration. I don't know what's going on, so I turn to substance abuse by drinking lots of wine and smoking joints, thinking that that's the way to help me get through this. What a joke. Let me tell you that trying to numb the pain by drinking more, and thinking I was still young by smoking pot (since our culture believes it's acceptable), was now my self-awareness. Marijuana doesn't work in the workplace, because it doesn't allow you to be aware that your actions and reactions impair your ability to see what your energy, your words, your reactions to problems presented, and what your actions mean to others. I couldn't think clearly because I clouded my perception and reality by not being in control of my responses.

You can't control the situation, but you can control how you react. I have always been a firm believer that acting is reacting. My acting mantra was going to be my silver bullet, so I started to maintain a neutral face and listen for the person's intention rather than simply their rejection of my requests. One thing I have learnt is not to take the practice of networking as a personal matter. That took me quite some time to manage by using positive self-talk when applying online for roles, not hearing back from former colleagues and contacts when requesting their insights, and feeling like time was my enemy because every day felt like Saturday, because nobody was in the office.

"I've learned how to adapt to different cultures and understand all different walks of life. I've also learned that confidence is key, even if you have to fake it at times. Fake it till you make it, as they say."
– Martha Hunt

There's that old saying again: "Fake it until you make it." That was the advice I used in order to cope with the voice in my head telling me that I wasn't good enough: I'm too old; I don't have the right education; I am going to be on the streets soon. Wow, the way we speak to ourselves is truly the reason for the increase in mental health illness in our society.

There were days when I would wake up and think that I was worthless and useless. I was depressed and feeling like no one cared if I lived or died. Also, I must admit that for the first time in my life, I began to wonder what life would be like if I wasn't here. My favorite Christmas movie is *It's a Wonderful Life,* by Frank Capra. I started to compare myself to George Bailey, who gave so much of himself to others that he had nothing left to credit himself for his positive influence he had on others in his life.

What could I do to put myself back into society? I wanted to check out, and I didn't know what that meant because I was just going through the motions of everyday life, expecting something to come along to revive my zest for life.

Positive perspective was needed to find an environment where I could be that fun-loving guy who is a very charismatic, very sincere, and honest individual who works diligently to make a difference. I was OK because I had the goods. However, I kept thinking I wasn't good enough, and that the game was over for me. I was failing. I was going to be the loser in this situation, even though I walked around acting like a winner. I felt like I was really losing it all the time, and I had to learn how to take control of myself again.

I recommend that when you look at your life, you don't reflect on a minute-by-minute, hour-by-hour, day-by-day horizon, but from a chapter-to-chapter perspective. Reflecting on the years when you felt you were your best self, what were you feeling at the time? I thought to myself that nothing worked better than when I was working constantly to prove myself, either through my ability to manage others or myself. I felt I was inspiring others to greatness, so I read self-help books, like *Awaken the Giant Within*, by Tony Roberts. It was my determination to feel the pressure to deliver an inspiring story for others seeking their next chapter, but I didn't know how to be my authentic self. Long ago, I decided to be authentic, because I grew up seeking to please other's needs. I was the good son. I was the good student. I was the good actor. I was the good guy. At the same time, I heard that good guys finish last. I thought to myself, *that's what's happening all the time for me.*

I never felt I was advancing in my search, because I was trying to prove myself in order to please others, in meeting business demands, developing their skills, and providing hope and encouragement for their futures.

Well, that's the joke, because I now know that if I can't make myself happy, nobody else can. I can't make everybody else happy, even though I may try really hard. I can't make anybody else happy unless I am happy with myself. I recommend journaling your feelings every day, and finding the patterns where you are unhappy with yourself. Journaling allows you to read your thoughts and recognize the feelings associated with them. The great Gandhi spoke for 2½ hours in front of parliament, explaining his quiet resistance. He didn't have any notes because he knew that you feel what you think, you think what you speak, and you say what you feel. I'm starting to feel happy because my plan to be worthy is working. I set and complete daily goals, I plan contacts weekly, I attend weekly networking groups, and I review my journal entries to identify my feelings of unworthiness.

I am excited that I am exactly where God wants me to be. I am real. I am better. I can be better. I am worthy.

Those are the hardest authentic words that I say to myself.

I am worthy despite the feeling that I am not worthy. I have now decided I'm going forward and being worthy to myself first, not proving my worth for others to see. That way, others will learn by my example, rather than my urge to teach people how to behave. I don't have to teach people how to learn. I don't have to teach people how to behave. This was a great discovery for me. I always thought, to be the leader, I had to be the role model who leads by example to be a good citizen.

There are set expectations in the workplace to be engaged and excited employees, and strong contributors, who exceed expectations so that they can be appreciated for their focus and energy, in the form of a performance bonus. I had set those expectations for others because I learnt that reward is supposed to differentiate one from others who don't meet performance objectives. I continued to be the driving force behind others so that they could learn something, perform tasks, increase knowledge, communicate effectively, and brand themselves for the company.

You learn things based on your own ability to associate with your previous process maps. Your brain functions with defined neuron pathways that are established based on your conditioning. Conditioning is how you learn to manage your behaviour, based on what is rewarded and what is not. I have been trapped within my own thinking that what you want to learn, or need to learn, is the principle of just-in- time training. My greatest discovery is that learning anything requires human kindness and will, because as I get older, I find it more challenging to replace existing process maps, within my brain, with new ones. The fundamental understanding in adult education is that we learn new information by how it relates to our current experience.

Today's society puts workers at a disadvantage, based on generational divides and the disposable nature that has become the new normal. Our society has been focused on personal gain, despite what happens to those in the community. It is getting difficult to have influence without learning new technology, new working approaches, new processes, new concepts, and new communication methods using social media. Also, we have set new expectations for when, where, and how we define work.

More and more, I realize that the focus is on just-in-time learning and just-in-time understanding of cooperation and collaboration to be good soldiers, rather than taking a stand for your beliefs and your perspectives backed by experience and education. What time is it for me, you ask? That's the question you must ask yourself. I'd learnt the most when I was doing something that was not simply watching a video, quoting a blog, or listening to a module that has no relevance to the business at hand. The gems of my experience that I have were acquired by just showing up. I have defined success as 10% knowledge and 90% determination. There is a 100% chance that by showing up these days, prepared for the multiple demands and distractions, can only be productive based on your personal goals that you want to accomplish. What you want to be known for, and more importantly, what you want to share with others, defines you as successful. I want to be known for being happy, energetic, and having exhilarating energy to make lives easier for those who want to learn to live without fear of the unknown.

I wish I knew this earlier, when people put me down with labels like being a *powerless suit*. I led a team of 83 people who looked to me for guidance, direction, and big picture understanding, by asking for process improvement approval while I listened to them to find ways to make them feel better about themselves and their efforts. The corporate environment encourages team successes. The matrix organization of most major companies wants to try to break down silos, even though we are taught to own our future state without communicating what that is. That's a contradiction, because teams are constantly changing and morphing; and this is because individuals don't get the loyalty or affiliation that working together once meant.

So now I am going out and promoting my accomplishments even though most of them were team successes. I found that concept hard to comprehend because I was conditioned to speak on behalf of team goals rather than personal achievements.

I never thought I would be able to boast or brag about myself, until I had to learn to promote myself to the degree that is expected today. It takes the understanding of human survival of the fittest, because our society is very focused on what we can accomplish without really being together. The workplace has become virtual reality versions of teamwork. You get hooked up to your screen and communicate via chats and emails. I thank God that I have some perspective of how to relate to others in society, which I knew as I was growing up, since I have been involved in theater productions as my passion. I have lead people through some tough challenges by sharing my love and commitment to those who have never experienced the teamwork required in producing a theatrical production. I have always associated leadership with sacrifice, because not everyone can be the *star*. What we accomplish together is far greater by the opportunity to impress people in working relationships created by love and respect rather than by money and individual gain.

I speak to my husband, and I talk about the thrill of the process whereby individuals give of themselves for the greater good, rather than simply for applause. The tireless efforts of those backstage are not acknowledged, but their generosity is expected. I have directed and acted in shows for the joy of seeing others' excitement and satisfaction of being vulnerable and open to feedback. For example, I stepped into the lead of a production during the final rehearsal week because the actor playing the lead, when he got his big break, decided his personal achievement mattered more than the other actors on stage. For another production, I moved sets and created a whole new environment when the original design didn't fit, based on poor construction advice.

During my work life, I designed and delivered onboard training programs without assistance from others, until the quality of the learning experience wasn't meeting the business demands. I bragged about myself to my husband, and yet I didn't know how to be that person who was grateful for opportunities, because it was expected that I could get the job done. I wanted others to like me to the point of exhaustion. The struggle for me was wanting to be liked. Nevertheless, I would tell others that I never want to be liked, but I wanted to be respected. I confused respect with love, because I thought to love was to respect somebody. When you are working to accomplish mutual goals, it doesn't mean you have to like those who work to accomplish the same. That's where I continued to have a crisis with my conscience, because I wanted everybody to like me more than respected myself.

Recently, I experienced a working relationship where I thought I was going to be loved and liked immediately by having to convince them that I knew everything, rather than relying on the existing management. Unfortunately, my ego suffered because I constantly acted as if I had all the answers, when I wasn't realizing that I hadn't earned anyone's trust in my abilities. That was a blow to my psyche because I have always earned trust in working relationships. I thought I hated those in management for being undervalued and unappreciated, but I was hating myself. I was forced to evaluate how to find the right fit for me and my *talents*.

Your personal brand is what people say about you when you're not in the room. I think by people seeing you smiling while you are working hard, masks that you're angry and frustrated by their lack of support. The signs for me were that I was anxious, despondent, and spoke aggressively, and I couldn't take the feedback that I scared people. I was oblivious to signs that pushing harder to be respected rather than liked doesn't make me very welcomed.

I now know that you can't always be liked.

People may like you for what they believe is what you do to support them based on their needs and wants. However, they will never respect you if you are seeking conformity rather than agreement on how to change their beliefs.

So, here I am, starting out again at 53, and realizing that I can do anything my heart desires. The only thing is that I have been doing everything in my life to be liked. Now I must understand how to like what I do, rather than seek others' approval.

That is deep. When I am constantly seeking approval from others, I don't know how to find my own way of approving myself. I still want to be liked for my ability to share my expertise, my experience, my skills, my energy, my influence, and my life. I have always liked my natural way to encourage others to think better about themselves. I want to be liked for taking everything that comes in life and making the best of it. It takes a lot for me to change my thoughts because I've always thought the worst of myself. I've thought that life is supposed to be difficult and a struggle. I've thought that life is supposed to be the time for working at what you can be compensated for rather than what you love. As a child, my father was one of those people that I admired with all my heart because he had such a tough life, with little education, but a tremendous drive to succeed.

My father was my hero because he consistently told me that I was good enough to accomplish anything if I worked hard. I worshiped him because I always felt that I wasn't good enough, because I didn't have the same skills that seemed to come naturally to him. I would follow him around and imitate his actions, his reactions, his persona, and his energy. He owned his own business since I was seven years old, so when I started to lead others at work, I would seek his advice, and he would say that people fire themselves when problems at work seemed overwhelming. He extended credit to anyone who would ask to earn their business. I knew it was because he was empathetic to people who needed help to get their car fixed to maintain their lives, even if they couldn't afford it. He was my hero, and after he died, I cried for three weeks. I didn't know how to be myself, because my biggest validator was gone. I had come to realize that my life was going to be a struggle, so I became an angry, frustrated, and aggressive individual. Thankfully, my father knew that I was going to get through this with the love and respect from my husband, Sean. The last piece of wisdom he gave me was when he held our hands and prayed that we would take care of each other. He said that he wasn't worried about leaving us behind.

I felt I had to be the patriarch by working my way up the ladder in the corporate world, for which I had aspired to be known as vice president someday. I charmed my way around people. Meanwhile, I pushed my way around my own husband, who would remind me that I was being my father, because I told him that was how I was taught to face life's challenges. What a lie I told myself in order to deal with his loss. I am glad to learn the lesson of how pushing people doesn't get you ahead of the game but rather away from them.

My world is about making choices every day to advance my spiritual understanding of my impacts on others. I have had days when I have awakened to do nothing, and still survive. However, being productive is about making goals, and working toward achieving those goals, to understand how I can approve of myself first. It is often said that our lives are stories that we tell others. Now I know that I must tell others about my understanding how to convey the bigger picture by my long-term relationship with God and, ultimately, with those he entrusts me to interact with in this world.

That's the *secret of life*, and that's why I'm here. In the next chapter, you will discover that I am operating under some great disillusions of how to behave in life.

Chapter 2: Learn How to Get Along With Others AGAIN

"It's hard to practice compassion when we're struggling with our authenticity, or when our own worthiness is off-balance."
– Brené Brown

2

I am making myself an authentic person. How many times have I said that to myself? I am going through life telling myself that I am honest, transparent, sincere, and forthright. So, that's a big deal!

I have realized that I am the exact opposite. I continue to worry about what others think of me. I am constantly comparing my skills and talents and thinking that I am not good enough. I am now realizing that I am working on how to explain my thoughts and my actions so that others can understand my intentions, my focus, and my determination. I have always projected myself as a caring and understanding person who seeks to understand everybody else's concerns but my own. I knew that I could understand how to help people to think differently, by essentially making them see their misunderstanding of issues and consequences of their actions. Until now, I know that I don't take criticism well because it affects me personally. I have constantly thought that being smart meant that I had to seek out examples when others did things that impressed me. Despite the fact, I may not have impressed them. Those who continued to shine amongst others or continued to demonstrate their efforts that made it easier for others to remove obstacles to become more productive, were my support. Whether at the office or directing a play, I recognized those who have thought through the process and determined how to improve it. I was grateful to others when I was working on a production, or if I was meeting others who shared my passion for the arts. I have always taken pride that I was being perfectly clear in my understanding when I was training and promoting skills for which I knew I had authority.

Now I have no authority over others. I am not thinking clearly, and people don't understand me. I am blaming it on how to listen properly for others' needs, wants, desires, expectations, and intentions. It's funny that I think I am a great listener by the way I listen. I consciously give others non-verbal affirmations— huhuh, mmm—while my head is nodding, and my face is neutral. Do you know how much work that takes? I am acting like I am listening when I am simply acting. I pretend to be listening, but I'm not hearing the words as I am formulating the next reply, the next brilliant wisdom I can share, the next life-changing response that will show others how I am intelligent and caring. All along, I was pushing people to deal with things as they came along, because I had the experience and the wisdom to point out their misunderstandings. I thought that my reason for being was to identify the sense of urgency of delivering the goods, just like the mailman. Talk about snail mail. I was acting like I was Professor Rabbit, who had just completed the four-minute mile, while anyone who was listening to me was receiving my messages like a turtle.

There is a great self-management technique that I have finally understood about communication: it isn't what you say that matters; it's what's heard. I have always listened to others while I was talking to myself. Imagine a conversation that doesn't have a speaker or a listener. Rather, a speaker, a listener, and *me. Me* is that voice inside my head that is constantly invading so I can add my two cents without hearing what the other person is saying. *"It's not what you say but how you make people feel,"* has never rang truer for me.

When I reflect on my work life, I think about what I did to make people feel they could trust me. I gave them the feeling that they could support me as I supported them, and the feeling that they knew me for being the best person every day, who could be relied upon for listening and caring about their needs. I know that setting goals is important, so focusing on what they aren't doing to reach their goals is what I think is expected of *Me* (that annoying little voice). I have been good at setting goals that align to business needs, performance outcomes, and professional development. In the corporate world, I would write my goals every year to ensure success, both personally and professionally.

I was able to work through the day-to-day issues, meeting those goals so that I felt that I was being productive. I am going through the process to truly listen with my spirit and not just my being. I am listening to understand the situations and pressing concerns, and the thoughts that are causing them. That is because of my findings in co-active coaching. I have discovered, from the book, *Co-active Coaching – The Proven Framework for Transformative Conversations of Work and in Life,* that I have been listening at a Listen I level: internal listening. I have been listening to my *Me* voice all the time, waiting for my turn to speak. Regardless of the situation or the concern being expressed by the other person, I have been waiting to speak from my perspective rather than hearing what is being said to me.

I have been told that I have a rubber face, and everyone can tell what I am thinking. I thought that was because I was being transparent, forthright, and honest as a person. Well, what honest person is thinking about themselves all the time? I remember once when I was listening to a colleague tell me about a conversation with his boss, about how he was going to improve the average call length by conducting side-by-side coaching. He was in pain because he hadn't been respected for his technical expertise but rather criticized for his good nature. I was incensed by the fact that I had previously reported to the same person as this colleague, and I wanted to conduct side-by-side coaching as part of my quality program tactics. I proceeded to say that it would never work, because I was wounded, thinking that it was my idea to have weekly, planned coaching sessions that would allow time to listen to a sample of calls, to coach by identifying observations in reference to patterns of observed behaviour. I wanted to use my expertise in devising clever conscious tactics to convince the employee to improve on the observed skill deficit. So, instead of encouraging my colleague to learn how to take observations and create plans for improvement, I stood there with my bitter face, and said, "Good luck, because the guy you report to doesn't understand the business." I was of no help at all to my colleague that day, even though I was a *good listener.*

Isn't a good listener someone who asks a lot of questions? Isn't a good listener someone who repeats or rephrases to let the speaker know he has been heard? Isn't a good listener someone who can connect ideas together for the speaker to gain clarity on the best response to questions? Isn't a good listener someone who doesn't interrupt others when they are searching to convey their thoughts? Isn't a good listener someone who can read emails, react to text notifications, plan for next conversations, and manage eye contact at the same time?

That's what the art of listening is about, isn't it? That's what I thought was the science of how the brain works. We are told that multitasking doesn't work; however, I am expected to stay focused and aware of how to stay prepared for what comes next. My *Me* voice is telling me that I will be a failure if I don't keep up with all the stimuli that is coming at me. So, what do others keep telling me?
SLOW DOWN.

Slow down is not a concept I expected to hear from others. We are in a fast paced, dynamic, and energized culture, where stimulants like caffeine, sugar, and carbohydrates are going to make you keep pace with others in the rat race.

Ah yes, the rat race. That is what life is all about. Well, I thought so anyway. I translated the rat race into the little mice on the wheel of life. We are little mice because I am a big believer in a story called *Who Moved My Cheese.* In the story, you have the mice, Sniff and Scurry, and the little people, Hem and Haw. Each of the characters relates to how we respond to change, and what that means in regard to what we want out of life. The way we respond to change defines our character, and that is the greatest lesson we can learn for the remainder of the years we are given to enjoy opportunities, share our love, and hope for a better future. I am proud to say that while I believed I was Haw, because I considered myself a change agent once the situation presented itself at work, I discovered that I was acting like Hem when my situation changed and I was no longer at work. I was dealing with the harsh reality that I was no longer a valuable member of society and wanted to make things stay the same prior to being released. I wanted to go back and apologize for my inability to accept the changes that were occurring. I wanted to show them that I was the skilled and flexible employee that they needed. I wanted to make them see that I could add great value to the organization, as it was not evolving as it is presently. I wanted to show them that I could lead others through the changes, when I wasn't able to look within myself to make the change that I needed to meet the new reality.

"Only I can change my life. No one can do it for me."
– Carol Burnett

The idea that engagement is not a connection, is really something that I'm struggling with currently. I thought I was always engaging people extremely well. I was acting like a wonderful, enthusiastic, and energetic person, to really get people to speak up and share their job search stories. I was treating all my encounters with others as if I was in training sessions, by asking a lot of questions to validate my understanding of what they know or didn't know about finding their next job. I'd ask a lot of questions to encourage participation in networking sessions. I would try to infuse my energy into the room so that people stayed focused and positive about the fact that another week had passed and no response to online job submissions had happened for me. I found sometimes that people were unfocused and negative about their job search, while I was applauding myself for being a good listener.

I thought I was improving my communication skills because I was listening with two ears. I was always a big fan of Judge Judy

Sheindlin, who proclaimed that God gave you two ears and one mouth for the reason of being a good listener. That way, I was showing that I was empathizing with everyone that I met, thinking that one day I was going to meet the *right* person who would locate the ideal job for my talents. What I realize now is that I was masking my inability to manage myself by trying to fix their perspectives. We have distractions in our lives that make it easier to procrastinate and not deal with our situations, and to blame others for what happens to us. I prided myself in helping people be focused and productive at work, when I was telling myself that people bring their baggage to work from their personal lives, which can get in the way. My experience in managing people to improve their skills meant distraction leads to lack of attention, which leads to lack of understanding of what's expected of you. I really wasn't connecting with people anymore but simply entertaining them. I was trying to keep them from falling asleep, because I wasn't sleeping properly. That was another reality that I was facing—the demons that come at night—the thought that I was never going to find a job again.

I was using my facilitator skills to look at things in order to be relatable to others that were suffering in silence like I was. It was a noble perspective because relating meant that people would trust me with their fears, and I could help them in their journey. I could help them see, hear, feel, smell, and taste differently. I wanted to engage the senses so that they could enjoy life again. When you are unemployed at a later stage in life, everything seems to feel as if you have failed. I had to be able to write a new story that would reflect my new reality. I'm thinking now that my ability to relate is more about what how people think within their own world. Their world is different from my world.

Trying to pretend I was able to figure out how my view of the world can align with others was my mantra. My training capacity was eager to evaluate whether the learner had learnt what you wanted them to experience. I translated my daily interactions as an opportunity to use my training skills, by randomly creating a learning objective based on my conversations with others I met while networking. I had been thinking I was being effective because this was the second time that I had found myself out of work.

I knew how to handle myself because I was being acknowledged by others in regard to how composed and prepared I was while participating in networking functions. I demonstrated my consistent and patient character, interacting as an enthusiastic and energetic person. I was not going to let others see that I was falling apart at the seams. What the other person understands about me and my abilities as a qualified trainer was going to be my brand. I'm trying to learn how to develop engagement skills that are relatable so that I can better understand myself. The journaling process is helping me realize that I am not as grounded and as great a communicator as I think I am. I'm not as concise as I think I am. I am not as clear as I think I am. I am not as professional as I think I am. I am trying to determine how that's impacting my success in finding the right fit for me. I want to be an example for people. I want to be a teacher. I want to be a facilitator. I want to be an instructor.

 When I speak with my family about the confusion and the pain I am feeling, they want to help, but they don't know how right now. My beautiful sister suggested that I teach French without a degree, because the school system is desperate for people who can manage a classroom. I think to myself that's the challenge for me. Then, I realize that there is no way I could manage a classroom of teenagers who would act like they are smarter and better than me. I am much too old for that!

I've set goals before, but now my goals become whatever anybody else thinks I can get paid to do. My daily routine has become looking to others to tell me how my life should unfold. I define myself by the desire that if I say the right thing to the right person, I will land a job. I need people to trust me again.

I find job search materials and share them willingly. I think that my passion for acting will help me land a job by doing a podcast on the pressures of job searching, and posting it on LinkedIn. I do this because I am told that sharing my perspective will attract others to my page and get them thinking about me. The great Uta Hagen, in *Respect for Acting*, says that acting is reacting. I am reacting to job searching, by being a voice for others who are afraid that their brand and reputation will be tarnished if they speak up for themselves. Confidently, I say that my reactions so far are not getting me my Oscar.

In real life, my Oscar will be won when I start seeking appreciation within myself. The self-worth will shine through when I learn how to get along with people again. It's funny that I'm sitting here alone in my apartment with my husband and my two cats, knowing I have a great life. I have a wonderful, loving relationship that has continued for over 25 years. Really, 50 years in a gay lifetime. I am a part of a great, loving family that continues to be there for each other. I want to be here for them. I have reframed my perspective in the way I want them to see that life's not fair. There are things like being released from my ideal role in a company that has wounded my pride. I was hurting because I was worried about what other people were thinking of me. I am learning that being there for my family, my friends, and a loving and respectful relationship is the legacy that I want on my tombstone. I want others to learn from my story so that I can earn that Oscar I have always desired. In the end, if knowing that I've helped people in their job search, and to continue their journey to being kinder to themselves, then I am sure that the next few years will bring a sense of accomplishment and security.

Chapter 3: How to Ask for What You Want (Art of Networking)

"One of the challenges in networking is everybody thinks it's making cold calls to strangers. Actually, it's the people who already have strong trust relationships with you, who know you're dedicated, smart, a team player, who can help you."
– Reid Hoffman

3

How to ask for what you want is the ART of networking. Like anything in art, it is a subjective experience that results in collective understanding. When I started networking, I was treating the exercise like a social interaction whereby I would ask to meet for a coffee or lunch, and recount how the individual and I were connected. I would try to relate to the person by walking down memory lane by reminiscing about when we worked together, when we shared a great past success, and when the good times were happening. Now, the good times are gone for me, and I am trying to maintain my positive persona and look to the individual for them to champion me internally within their company. Asking people for help never came easy for me because I felt it represented weakness. I was worried that others would take pity on me, and that I would leave the conversation feeling sad and depressed, thinking that another day had passed and no job. My ME voice was telling me to laugh and smile, while inside I was begging for them to take me into their office and proclaim that I was going to solve their problems. I know that sounds crazy, but it was the way I was feeling.

It has taken a lot of positive self-talk to convince myself that everyone goes through the same feelings of being up and down during this process. Sometimes the worry I had was that I was depending on others for my future. I prided myself on being the leader, the independent voice who spoke for others when they came to me to solve their problems. I was acting like the professional who wasn't asking for help but rather offering my opinion based on the recent LinkedIn posting that I had read, or the networking discussion that I had. I have since learnt that asking for help isn't the way to gain confidence in yourself; rather, it is telling them that you are working toward your goals. People are more impressed to hear that you are working on building your skills and gaining knowledge about your industry, and working to be a more marketable entity when they champion you within their circle of influence. We are expected to be productive and produce things, and address our weaknesses and build on our strengths, so that we are ready to solve the problems that are presented before us. I tell myself I am grateful for the time to work on myself, because when I am working again, I may not get the chance to take courses, read books to build my resources, or try to learn something new. Unfortunately, I would boast about all the wonderful learning I was doing, when actually, I was depressed and forlorn that I couldn't concentrate on spelling my name half the time. I think the loneliness was causing me to be unfocused, because I didn't have tasks to schedule or projects to complete.

That loneliness is something that truly defines my character. I am learning to like being alone, without feeling lonely. That is a huge development for me because I have always surrounded myself with people; because I was an overweight child who relied on TV for friendship.

I think you can relate that when you are at work and you are meeting deadlines, fulfilling your calendar commitments, and coordinating efforts with colleagues, the time flies. The hardest thing for me is managing my time when I don't have someone else to hold me accountable. Now, I must be accountable to myself. So, I begin to use my google calendar and schedule time to work on finding a job. The adage, *looking for a job is a full-time job*, becomes my company's vision. I am going to find the right job by putting in the time to update my resume, do personality tests to see how I can transfer my skills, and sign up for multiple aggregators, for fear of missing opportunities. All the time, I am being trained by transition counselors that the right jobs aren't posted on Monster, LinkedIn, Zip Recruiter, or some other job listing posted on the internet. I need to find individuals, within the companies that I am targeting, who will tell me what is available by my sharing of what I want to do. The inevitable question, "What are you looking for?" is the trigger for which I must play the role of confidant and define what I can do to solve the problems the individual feels is happening in their organization.

I am looking at networking as the opportunity to check out which companies I don't want to work for. I am listening for poor management, broken team communication, and the overworking of people's energies and spirits. Networking becomes a filtering process to not get the chance to work somewhere. All the while, I am using my interpersonal skills, and my relationship and my communication skills, to feel like I am still working. I think to myself that my skills are still viable based upon the expectation that someone will say to me, "Wow, you are good enough for me to recommend without being afraid that you will tarnish my reputation." I guess that was my biggest misconception, since I have been promised that persistency pays off when networking. However, my chance of landing the right job isn't going to happen unless I am in front of a hiring manager. My fears are growing as I am putting my faith into the process of networking by promoting my skills to someone who has no influence in the hiring decision process. I soldier on, promoting myself to gather information that I can use to show that I am remaining current in the industry, preparing to hit the ground running without hesitation, and I am still young enough to be considered for growth, upon being hired.

Thinking for others starts to be my way of being. It feels uncomfortable speaking to recruiters, because you get thirty minutes to impress someone with your attitude, your experience, and your personality, to move forward in the hiring process. I start to think that I am in control of the situation by using the tactics that are recommended by others who have successfully found the right job. I practice my responses to possible interview questions so that I don't sound rehearsed when I speak with recruiters. I research companies so that I can show interest in their vision and values, based on the conversations that I have had while connecting with the person who champions me to obtain the initial recruiting interview. I think to myself that I must submit hundreds of resumes and template cover letters to get one or two interviews a month, if I am lucky. I am thinking for others when I ask how I can help them in their daily lives. Networking does work, but it takes time, and I am thinking that time is running out.

This is when the feeling of being out of control is happening. Thinking that I am in control when I am meeting with someone to say I am available for any opportunity, I am hiding my desperation to be liked and wanted by asking how I can help them. What's happening to my self-respect? When will the meetings, the promises, the hopes, and the dreams of finding the right job finally come to pass for me? When will I hit the jackpot and be considered worthy again? I am now realizing I am suffering from low self-esteem. Those close to me, such as my husband, my family, and my friends can see that I am hurting, but they don't know what to do for me.

I am shutting down, and nothing is going as planned. The plan is that I will find the right job within six months. Well, six months comes and goes, and there are no offers on the table. I am clinging to the hope of being the lucky one who gets hired in their fifties. I am still hoping that I will be worth the compensation I believe I am worth. I am eager to get back to work to stop the negative thoughts of failure and hopelessness.

I am seeking opportunities to find some enjoyment out of all this so I that I am in the right frame of mind to conduct training classes without terrifying the participants with my crazed thoughts. I am using my acting skills to really focus on my learner experience, so I get the chance to demonstrate my blended learning strategy in networking.

I take on the role of learner, since I know that people learn things by reading articles, blogs, watching modules, applying practice exercises, speaking with other people to learn from their experience, and seeking mentors for feedback.

I was targeting a company with which I have a long-term relationship. I was the client of this company for over twenty years and had gained deep knowledge of their systems, their processes, and their business models. I was working all the contacts I had internally to get a Learning Consultant role within their Learning and Development team. I met with the hiring manager and connected with her by dropping names of vice presidents, managers, and staff that I had contacted to be considered for the interview. I was happy that the interview went well. We spoke for over an hour, and I was told that the job was going to be working on a learning authoring tool, so I should teach myself how to use it. I was in consideration for the role, because I was informed that another interview would be scheduled, with an assignment. Unfortunately, I was not thinking clearly because my fears of being not good enough caused me to procrastinate and spend practically no time learning the authoring tool. I had sabotaged myself because I was waiting to get the assignment as my excuse to not teach myself the tool. I was given the assignment at 4:30 PM the previous evening, to present the impacts of blended learning at 10:00 AM before the team in which I would be working. I thought to myself that I could do this, because I had been using a blended learning approach while I was playing the role of learner in my job search. I was in a panic state, blaming myself for not learning how to use the authoring tool. After about three hours of trying to teach myself how to build the presentation, I went online and grabbed slides from other presentations on the subject, without knowing how I could present the material without looking like a blithering fool in front of the team.

After bragging about putting together training curriculums, I tried to put together a PowerPoint presentation with lots of interactivity built within it. I was going to really focus on keeping them engaged in the room with my sparkling personality and charming demeanor. I was hoping that my energy and enthusiasm would win them over since that was the way I was conducting business while I was looking for a job. I am tap dancing (without the shoes) around the room because I am using my body, my hand gestures, my eye contact, my smile, and my dynamic facial expressions to subside my feelings of not being prepared for the interview. I was waving my arms and swaying back and forth, because my ten-year-old clunky computer wasn't working, while I was trying to load the presentation that I had "lovingly" pulled together. What a sight I must have been. You guessed it, I didn't get the role. I did impress the company recruiter, who gave me the feedback that I wasn't the right fit for the team. However, the art in networking was that the same recruiter contacted me weeks later, with another opportunity to use my facilitation and relationship management skills to work within another team that was launching a new role to meet increasing business demands.

I am off to the races, and I convince myself that I am targeting the right company. So now I need to put more energy into preparing for the upcoming interview with the hiring manager. I knew the individual who was doing the hiring, from a previous working relationship, so I believed she would think I was the perfect choice for the role because of my knowledge of their systems.

I impressed the vice president of the company during my interview, by highlighting facts, figures, and stories to gain her support. It appeared that I was overqualified, so she focused on the fact that the compensation for the role was much lower than I was asking. Remember that *overqualified* means that you are too expensive for them, since they can hire a younger individual at a lower price. I convinced her that I could be flexible and appreciate any opportunity to work at the company, as I had been targeting it for six months. It looked like I was nearing the finish line, because I was speaking with the partnering team overseas, to whom I would be facilitating new business processes and procedural training. I was excited that the two women with whom I was speaking were laughing and enjoying my deep understanding of the business. I was impressing them with my ability to concisely describe some of the solutions I was proposing, to develop our working relationship, because I was the right fit. I even regaled them with some of my travel stories, since the role required international travel, and my maturity and cosmopolitan lifestyle would make me the ideal candidate. I didn't get the job. Now, how do I handle being rejected again within the same month? I discovered that there had been an internal, younger candidate, with international experience, who had been working on the team, who was promoted to the role.

Oh well, the ART of networking is not like science when preparation isn't all that is needed.

I had appreciated the feedback that the recruiter had provided me, but still, my networking days aren't over.

I started to seek feedback from my network to better understand how to position myself for my new and improved 90-second elevator speech. The experience of nearly winning the right fit has provided me great insights as to how to speak with people that I haven't connected with yet. I am facing my fears of seeking help by reaching out to all those that have the Learning Consultant or training titles within industries outside my comfort zone.

The next step in networking is approaching individuals with whom I have had some form of relationship within my lifetime.

I have been performing in community theatre productions for over twenty years, so I started to think that any of those individuals would be sympathetic to my situation and offer to help.

There is a time when you start to believe that you can do anything that you find interesting, appealing, and fun, because the targets that you set are not working. The targets I chose were within the financial services industry because that was where I had spent most of my career. So now I am looking outside my industry by believing that my transferable skills in people management, call center management, relationship management, and training and facilitation management will be easily transferred to other industry opportunities. Notice that the word, *management*, keeps coming up while I am trying to manage myself, and that's not going well. I am seeking feedback from others so that I can position myself within other industries, like a chameleon who can apply and pretend to be the right candidate. Meanwhile, my self-esteem is running at its lowest. I am working out, determined to stay young looking, and I am convincing myself that I can learn the business like a freaked-out bunny rabbit on speed when I get the interview. I am doing research by combing the internet to gain the instant knowledge needed to be able to associate my previous experience with what is happening in the company for which I have connections but no expertise. *Expertise* implies that you are an expert in the field that you plan to pursue, not *simply land the job and pretend to be an expert*. I was fooling myself to believe that I could *fake it till I make it*.

Please remember that when you are networking with others who are networking to land a job, the feeling of anything places you in a dream state. I was dreaming that I could walk into any interview and walk out saying to myself that I needed the experience of interviewing to get the *right* job. In the meantime, I was trying to appeal to anyone who was willing to give me 30 minutes of their time to just be considered hireable.

I am meeting with people that I have connected with via LinkedIn, Facebook, networking groups, and friends and former colleagues to seek their feedback as to what and where I should be focused. I am staying positive by being careful to sound positive and not allow myself to speak badly of my former working relations, for fear of retaliation. I am acting like I can apply my skills to earn their trust to recommend me for roles that I have not considered in other industries, to feel like I am making progress. I am starting to think that I can do anything if I fit the suit. That's an old acting mantra that I have heard in the past: that you can get hired in films and TV by fitting into the costume. It doesn't matter if you have any skills, because the camera will make you look like you *fit*. Now I am willing to put on any costume in hopes that I may find the *right fit*.

Unfortunately, this strategy is making me dislike myself, because I know that my fraudulent actions are not getting me interviews but are taking me further away from the *right fit*. What is the *right fit* again? I start questioning if there is a *right fit*.

I am now coming up to seven months without working, and my family is worrying about me. My mother tells me that I am too old to be out of work this long. I need to go out and find a job like everybody else. I need to put more energy into finding a job and stop wasting time meeting with people. I need to remember that I don't have as many working years as I used to have, she tells me. I need to be more like my siblings who are working despite the fact they are not liking where and what they are accomplishing.

Wow, some feedback can really hurt.

I am getting more depressed by drinking more heavily and numbing myself with marijuana at night to attempt to get some sleep. I am seeking the support and feedback of others, but I don't know how to take criticism, which I am reminded of by my partner. Thankfully, he is a man of principles and kindness, and he kept himself away from me by working more flights as a flight attendant, to keep his own sanity as I am losing mine.

I found that I was creating a job for myself, because I was treating my search as a job. I was scheduling myself by learning when I would expect a response from the over forty applications that I had submitted online. I asked others in networking groups how many applications they had submitted, and I hear stories of from 10 to over 100 applications, so I think that I need to find out how to send more. One of the missing links is that I don't know how to follow up with the forty applications that I have submitted over the preceding six months, because I try to reach out to the talent acquisition people who represent the companies for which I have applied, by using LinkedIn premium service. I hadn't heard any response from the InMail service, which is supposed to be the reason you use the premium service—like it's going to matter that you are spending about $40 a month just to be considered among the other hundreds of emails that they probably get a day. The days keep coming, and my VISA bill keeps growing. What next?

I am working on finding more opportunities to register myself with more job aggregators that fill my inbox with lots of job postings. I am spending 3 to 4 hours a day trying to see what other industries I can see myself in, as well as my own. I use a template cover letter that I have been trained to use by the transition company, so that I can send out something that looks professional as opposed to the cover letter saying I am over 50 but can still be the best employee you know.

My thoughts keep reminding me that the *right fit* is the hidden opportunity that doesn't get posted, and that someone internally is going to take the resume and cover letter from my online submission, and make my dream come true. My heart is yearning, but my head is telling me that I am among thousands of others who are thinking the same.

I can't blame people for trying to find people who are younger, as I did the same thing when I was in a hiring capacity. I keep telling myself that hiring the right person takes time, and that I may be the lucky one that gets noticed by my clever cover letter template and my experience in managing teams. Hey, everyone is on a team these days, so my luck is running out, right? However, now I am relying on luck to get an interview, as I have no one I know to recommend me within in companies in other industries. What's the best way to get noticed by people who don't know you? Use social media.

I am posting my thoughts and observations to articles and adding comments to get noticed by former colleagues and friends, to help me find hidden opportunities that exist within companies that aren't targets anymore. My targets seem to have dried up, so I am hoping that others will lead me to companies that I can approach with my new-found transferable skills approach. I am building a network of people by searching others' profiles, to send invitations to connect in order to possibly meet them, in hopes of making my presence known. However, I don't have any past experiences that I can reflect on and recollect, so I stay up to date with current events in hopes that I can strike up an intelligent conversation about business, politics, popular culture, or social media posts. All the while, I am playing nicely with them so that they don't think that I am seeking them out for something. I have never been a person to *kiss ass* for what I wanted, but now I am taking that path, and it feels shitty.

This process is not winning me a lot of friends, because my time horizon to engage them is right now, while theirs is occupied with things like working. When you're working, you don't necessarily check social media as often as I am doing. My transition coach is advising me that people check their social media in the morning, at lunch, or on the weekends. Mondays are not available because people are getting their minds focused on their weekly activities. Thursdays are when pressing things are slowing down, or perhaps in the evening, when you're opening emails or invitations instead of deleting them based on the subject line or person that you don't readily know. Everyone has their busy lives based on their business at hand. As job opportunities are presenting themselves by the multitude of aggregators that I have *working* for me, I am neglecting the 25 to 50 target companies that I originally started on my search. Luckily, I am still getting pushes from the targeted companies, based on my profiles that I have created, which advise me of matches to my skill set, so I have some relief when some appear in my inbox.

I reflect on what those databases tell me about the newly posted opportunities, so I start the hunt for people within the company who are key influencers. My biggest problem was that I was looking for people who were either at my level or maybe below my level within the companies, thinking that they would be willing to connect. I was afraid to send out a promotional package with a video, podcast, or other clever marketing item to grab the attention of executives who may have influence on the hiring decision makers. I was coached to know that presidents of the company can be used to get in the door, since they have lots of issues, and people seeking their attention and approval. Unfortunately, I started suffering with *old man syndrome*, because those people were younger, smarter, and more attractive than I was feeling about myself.

I needed something funky so that I could compete with this new generation of job seekers. I joined a team of job seekers to develop a podcast, to illustrate the proper way of networking so that I could tell the world that I was vibrant and had a younger thinking perspective. I taught myself how to use the technology that everyone I spoke with seemed to already know. I wanted to embrace technology that would say that I could be hired because I could keep up with the times. Thankfully, I found kinship in another job seeker who was older than me, so I could act like the guide to feel that I wasn't too ancient in my thinking. I soon found that working with other job seekers meant I was dealing with hidden agendas, fears, and prejudice, which made the process far lengthier than anticipated, and resulted in a very poor product that I reluctantly posted on LinkedIn but never shared with those influencers I was trying to reach.

I'm back to feeling I had to be liked rather than respected for my project management and training skills. I am thinking that I may not ever find the *right fit*, because I don't understand how to fit into this new world of work.

I began my research to see how the government could assist me financially to get myself around others who know and understand how to operate in the world. That was a dead end because I am informed that I am overqualified and have earned too much in the past to qualify for the programs. I have never been a racist, but now I am being discriminated by being a white, middle aged, able-bodied man.

The power of networking finally starts to work when I connect with somebody I haven't spoken with in 20 years. The funny thing is that our connection wasn't the fact that we were both seasoned training professionals but that we had been in a musical. He advised me that he was leaving his position, and that judging by my experience on my LinkedIn profile, I would be a great candidate for his job. The gods have spoken, and my scattered brain was finding relief. The only hurdle next was to convince his boss that I was the *right fit*.

He arranged the interview for me, for which I am eternally grateful. I assured his boss that I have the transferable skills in a training capacity, and that my inquisitive and knowledge seeking nature would fit perfectly within his team. I gained his support and went on to the interview with the president of the company. I am personable, knowledgeable, and know lots about their purpose and positioning within the fundraising industry, since I have been gathering information from charitable group websites. I impressed him with my engaging spirit and willingness to provide leadership courses to meet their growing culture of inclusiveness and diversity. We discussed ways to improve the culture to serve his clients with more meaningful interactions and make fundraising sales easier. Everything was going my way!

We agreed to the compensation that I was seeking, as well as the position on the management team, which I believed would allow me to make a difference. I was excited, because my mantra through this journey was *find the right fit,* where I could make a difference rather than just get a paycheck. The verbal offer was accepted, and I was on my way.

Then, I got the written offer, sent to me via email, and all that was discussed had been altered by the Human Resources department, which was explained to me as being because I don't have direct fundraising experience. I was crushed.

I asked to renegotiate the conditions of the offer, only to be advised that they had decided to defer the position until they could assess the need for the role upon my friend's departure.

That is the ART of networking: surviving the highs and the lows of expecting the best for yourself based on conversations, and maybe getting the worst when offers are presented.

Chapter 4: Think Before You Speak (Power of Making a Great First Impression)

"Think twice before you speak, because your words and influence will plant the seed of either success or failure in the mind of another."
– Napoleon Hill

4

I am sharing some personal perspectives to provide insights into how to manage yourself when you think that you have already learned everything by now. I think that people look to someone who has turned 50 as someone who should know better. I should know how to be productive every day. I should know how to be respectful of others. I should know the business for which I am searching for my next opportunity. I should know how to present solutions that others can embrace. I should know how to be an effective communicator. I should know what acceptable behaviour in the workplace is. I should know how to improve the culture, the processes, the protocols and the practices, because I have all the experience that is on my resume. I should know how to negotiate with others to gain their interest in how to work more effectively. I have been planning and dreaming of the chance to make a difference again.

As I start to feel that I was being heard, I start to speak more. I was under the impression that hiring the right person took time because the hiring manager was searching for the right fit within their team, their company, and their culture. Culture is a funny thing because it evolves with every new person who joins the company. They are the unwritten biases, the secrets that people are willing to share about the working conditions that are written in a mission statement. The culture is dictated by the values that are written by senior management, without any of the employees' consent. My full-time job in finding the right job is to ask my network contacts about the culture of the company that I am targeting, so that I make the right choices every day of how much energy to spend on finding the right culture fit for me.

It's easier to shake off cultural influences when you are younger, because you haven't had opportunity to shape the culture. A twenty/thirty something is still learning the business of the industry they are in, to not care about the culture in which it operates. When you are searching for the right culture to fit you, you are thinking about what your last culture that you worked in was like, since that is the only frame of reference you have. You hope to find familiar management styles, a familiar pace, familiar social interactions, familiar colleagues, and familiar faces. Usually, you are seeking all the familiarity because you are reaching out to people who you have known in past circumstances, and you trust that they will give you the information to make the right choice to join their company.

I am an extrovert, so I am seeking out those to help me understand about the working culture so that I can apply for the jobs that are the *right fit* for me. I am at a stage in my life where I don't want to waste time working in a culture that is not comfortable, challenging, and rewarding enough for me to live out my last 15 years of working life. Besides, I have come this far believing that I was going to remain at my last company for the rest of my productive, healthy, and happy life. Now I am trying to regain the same feeling of being in a tribe of people that values the same things that I do.

Here I am, working at improving my training and facilitation skills by setting goals to be ready for the next job offer. I enlisted the help of a mentor who encourages me to think about performance consulting. I have always considered myself to be the person who initiates new ways of thinking and doing better on the job, based on my 20+ years in leading teams of administrators and call centers within financial services operational units. I have naturally used my determination to exceed strategic goals, and I have sought out individuals who can use their strengths in being organized and goal driven to train others by sharing concepts, system navigational tips, and their knowledge. I have been using my intelligence to gain experience on handling customer complaints and use cases to improve the current processes and procedures to manage risks. I am constantly looking for feedback on how to motivate others to bring forth their insights into making the customer experience a priority. Now I am ready to understand what all my talents are leading me to do. Performance consulting sounds right for me.

After not getting interviews for about a month, I sought to understand how performance consulting could be the life for me. I researched multiple books and discussed my findings with my mentor. I was excited to be talking business again, and the need to express my intelligent perspectives was moving me forward daily. I was eager to learn how to use my new-found identity to position myself as a consultant who can analyze the strategic goals and provide observations as to why and how team and individual performance can meet them. I could use my call center management expertise to enhance management practices and meet performance objectives that are not meeting strategic goals. I could use my people and relationship management skills again. Hooray!

As my confidence grew, I started to comment on LinkedIn articles about employee satisfaction measures and tips. I registered for webinars, focusing on training practices that provide techniques to leverage current practices, providing a blended learning approach. I read about ways for improving call center practices, which I could share when I land my dream job doing performance consulting. I envisioned myself entering an organization being heralded as a prophet who could implement the plan to prove I was worthy of being hired. I was still wanting to be the leader I had previously thought I was being. My self-esteem felt like it was coming back, so I believed the *right fit* for me was just waiting to appear. My George Bailey voice was loud and clear: "I WANT to live again."

This new motivation and determination to lead others to managing their problems comes from hours of doing research in the library. I convinced myself that applying the techniques I was reading about would allow me to learn as I go, by applying my existing experience with my newly developed knowledge base. I was reading with such veracity, and taking notes, because I thought I was running against this large clock. Some of you may remember the game, *Beat the Clock*, where contestants were given some embarrassing tasks that they had to do to beat the clock and win the prize. Often, there were stupid stunts to make people look like imbeciles and that they were incompetent. That was how I was behaving, as if I needed to prove to the world that I wasn't incompetent and an imbecile. I took notes and visualised situations where I could apply my wonderful wisdom that I was gaining. I was loving myself for taking the time to upgrade my skills by reading and consuming all that I could within the schedule that I had set for myself. Now I am going around claiming to be a performance consultant because I needed to narrow my focus and know how to identify my talent. Throughout my career, I was open to any challenge to improve myself by telling myself I could do that without pursuing any education, because I used my common sense and personality to meet the challenge. I am still taking the same approach, but now I don't have any measure of success. There aren't any people guiding me or informing me if I am doing a good job. I am seeking roles where I can use my *educated* wisdom to impress recruiters and hiring managers, so that I can hit the ground running in whatever industry happens to think I am the *right fit*. That's how I am feeling. There is the desperation that time is passing me by, and I had better get educated because every posting I see requires a degree of some kind, and I don't have one. I was looking around, hoping to be liked again for being the mature and seasoned worker; however, I wasn't feeling very professional anymore.

I constantly prepare myself by scripting answers to interview questions that will highlight my performance consulting talent, so I am believable when I am speaking with confidence for my network contacts and hopefully during interviews. I am in control again, and I am loving it!

My confidence makes it sound like I know what I am talking about. I meet people and pass out my cards with assurance that I am The Service Training Guy. I am thinking that my clever forthright descriptor of me will get me noticed, and roles will flourish, because now I can market myself to anybody who will listen. I don't consider what impacts I have on others listening about how I can solve their servicing complaint problems. I am so self-centered that I became the *authority* on service delivery, because I have the goods now. I enrolled to become certified as a training development professional because I am ready to be validated, and I seek to put letters behind my name to prove it! All the while, I am putting more money on our credit card, because to earn the credits I am craving, I must pay for them.

Unfortunately, my husband is not seeing the game plan because I only share bits and pieces for fear of losing him, because I know that he is worried about our finances. Nevertheless, I am working to become credible. I am ignoring him because I know that I am determined to get my designation and get my dream job, and because now I am qualified to put my cherished letters on my resume to pass the key word search—the dreaded key word search!

You must understand that today's job market is flooded with candidates that are considered for their education credits as opposed to experience. Technology has taken away the opportunity for hiring managers to review resumes, because you can see that thousands of people view job postings within days of posting. They rely on recruiting software to filter out the qualifications of candidates. The internet has provided opportunity for individuals to apply for any job, regardless if they have the qualifications or experience in the field. Today's practice of filtering out online applications, based on matching job descriptions to resumes showing the same words, means I must customize my resume to match the words in the job description. I think that leads me to be a fraud, because I don't have the will to claim to have earned something I haven't. My heart is telling me to stay true to myself and have one resume as opposed to variations to *fit the suit.*

My approach is to use the same resume but customize my cover letter so that my personality stands out. I hope to wow the company recruiter with some cleverly crafted introduction to grab their attention and pray that I am not filtered away by the software. Wake up, this is not going to work! After weeks of not receiving any responses from my weekly online applications, I decide that I need to seek feedback from a couple of trusted friends in my network, to adjust my resume to match keyword searches, because I feel if I can't beat them, I am going to join them.

Off I go to start my new strategy of positioning myself based on the variation of about three types of resumes. First, I have my standard version, which consists of details of my accomplishments so that I can highlight my call center management experience. The second one consists of a training and facilitation focus, to ensure that I exemplify my talents and qualifications as a trainer that can easily fit into any organization regardless of industry. I can show that I can easily transfer my skills, because of my amazing ability to work with subject matter experts and gain agreements from stakeholders on projects. Lastly, my third one is a combination of management and training, to reflect the fact that I can readily assume a people management role that requires training, coaching, and performance management, since I have always been recognized for those skills based on advancing with my former employers. This is going to knock the socks off anyone who takes the time to read three pages. Oh no, I think to myself that I am going against the grain, because everyone knows that you are lucky if people read beyond the first page these days. What kind of strategy is this?

Nevertheless, I am armed and ready for any call, text, email, or network contact who expresses any interest in speaking with me about my future. I charge on with confidence, thinking that after about seven months of search, I finally know how to play the game. Too bad there isn't an instruction manual that I could locate so I wouldn't have wasted half the year searching aimlessly without the proper ammunition. I am speaking to people with authority because I have learnt how to do my job. Remember, finding a job is like having a job, so I am well beyond my six-month learning curve. Hooray for me, because I am going to get a *"meets expectation"* on my performance review. The only thing is, there isn't anyone to evaluate my progress but myself. So, I give myself a passing grade, with some positive self-talk that I am now worthy to be considered for anything that happens to spark my interest.

My approach has changed from using my network contacts to champion me to put my resume in front of hiring managers, to applying to roles that I think would be fun, like working for the Ontario Lottery Corporation, where every day would be like working in a casino. I had been to Las Vegas for my fiftieth birthday celebration, with eight friends and family members, so I can certainly qualify for how to behave in a highly charged casino establishment. Woo hoo!!!

Now I am on my journey to find the right fit, and I feel empowered to locate my next opportunity, with this sense of self-pride because I have learned what I need to be my best self. Oh, so I tell myself that every day. I don't really know what I am doing, but I convince myself that scouring job aggregators for hours at a time will bring me luck, and I can use my intelligence to win my internal battles. I believe that I am handling my fears better because I am drinking less and working out more, although I'm not sleeping well because I can't shake my fear that time is passing me by. So, I use marijuana more at night to feel tired and lethargic in order to want to go to bed. I am feeling angry with myself because I know that smoking more is going to increase my risks of getting heart disease and perhaps suffering a stroke. However, my mantra is that if I am going to abuse my body, I must use it to counter any disease. I started my new regiment of eating less processed foods and setting up a daily workout schedule, including increasing my time on the elliptical to improve my cardiovascular system. I am determined to look healthy despite abusing my body with nicotine and drugs. I started drinking four cups of coffee a day to keep up my energy and enthusiasm, and to mask the fact that I am not sleeping more than four hours a night. I become anxious and agitated to the point where my words and my attitude towards my husband are abusive, aggressive, and irritating. He continues to try to encourage me, but I know that I am pushing him away; and in my heart, I know I wouldn't want to be around anyone who was acting the same. Luckily, he has taken the vow of for better or worse, and for richer or for poorer, and he reminds me of them when I ask why he hasn't left me yet.

My words at home come from anger and frustration, but my words outside the home come from the need to socialize with others. I think to myself that this is what work/life balance is not supposed to be about. Nonetheless, I am operating like a well-oiled machine that is destructive rather than constructive. I have always been a person that doesn't think first before speaking, because I feel the need to apologize for how I have made others feel bad. I have never maliciously tried to hurt others, but my vocabulary and perspective have caused me to reflect after speaking about the impact I have made.

I try breathing exercises and mindfulness techniques to train myself to think before I speak. Truly, I don't know how to practice them because I have put myself on a treadmill of caffeine and nicotine, which causes me to have heart palpitations that worry me at night. I think to myself that all this will go away as soon as I find the *right fit*. I can't believe how unfocused I was, when I believed that I was gaining focus because I was studying for my certification three to four hours daily so I could meet my goals. Time is ticking, and I am heading to the finish line. The only thing is that I keep moving the finish line, since I keep thinking that I am being destructive despite my constructive schedule I have set for myself.

Talk about Beat the Clock?

Now, you must remember that I was on this treadmill before, after being released from working at a company for 18 years. Then it took about 18 months to land my next job, so I am determined to reduce that time by half; it's just that I don't have control of the universe, even if I think that I do!

In the meantime, I am training myself to breathe and listen for cues when I am speaking with friends and network contacts, to appear to be in control. I work myself every day by putting my energy towards feeling better about the situation, and by convincing myself that this too shall pass. I want to be liked again because I am hating myself, so I seek out volunteer opportunities and reach out to a gay sponsored group to share my training skills based on a network contact. Now, you must think I am running on empty when I hope to be inspired to work with young professionals who are championing the cause, to provide resources and support to combat prejudice against newly graduated, openly gay professionals in the corporate sector. I have always hidden my sexual orientation for fear of reducing my chances to advance my career; hence, I have fooled myself into thinking nobody knows. Thankfully, I have shared my amazing 27-year committed relationship (16 years married) with my theatre friends and acquaintances, to feel *normal* as I climbed the corporate ladder. It gave me great pride when people would be amazed at how long we have been together. You see, gay men are criticized for being promiscuous, so we would joke that our marriage was better than most straight ones. We were the lucky ones who were going to make it no matter what!

I am on track to finding my next job, because I am starting to get people responding to me for interviews. This means that I am getting noticed and I am on fire! See what happens next as I come closer to finding my *re-purpose*.

Chapter 5: How to Love What You Think You Love

"If you don't love what you are doing, it could be misery."
– Dakota Fanning

5

This time in my life represents a privilege and a curse. My privilege is that I have made enough money not to be afraid of not working every day, and the curse is that I haven't made enough money to live the life I had envisioned. I have lived many years of strategic planning; I was going to save enough money that I would be free of having to punch a clock after sixty. Now, I am afraid that I will be punching a clock until I am 80! That is the greatest lesson that I have learnt during the transition from one job to another: how to deal with the anxiety of not having enough money. At first, the idea of being unemployed creates the feeling of being broke. When you are broke, you lose your passion, your drive, and your enthusiasm for the future. You constantly worry if there will be enough to sustain today, and tomorrow seems like an eternity. I have always been a person with a passion for life. My mantra has been that life is to be lived, not to be endured. Now I am struggling to endure the next five minutes! So, what has happened to my passion?

Learning to talk to myself as a kind, caring, and understanding individual when I am working and producing is one thing, but try doing it when my ME voice is saying that with each passing day, the passion for life continues to drift farther away. I am now listening to my ME voice, which is envious of those around who are accomplishing goals, being appreciated for their talents, and travelling to experience the many pleasures of life. I am resentful when hearing about friends taking vacations, former colleagues advancing in their careers, and family members planning for life events like Christmas, New Years, weddings, birthdays, and get-togethers. I am ashamed that I am in my fifties and thinking that my life is stalled, when everyone else's is still in motion. My passion for the theatre is my only outlet, and even that seems to be too costly for me to enjoy. I worry about spending money on seeing shows or plays. I know that we can't afford to spend savings from the last 30 years, because I am uncertain as to when I can build them up again. All the time, I am feeling this passion dying inside me, and I want to blame the people who put me in this state of mind. I am secretly hiding this desperation by not associating with anyone in my network that relates to my former employer, so I am cutting off a lot of my essential contacts. I prepare for interviews, wondering how I can make claim for my success stories if I don't have anyone who witnessed the impacts they made, to back them up. However, I convince myself that this approach is going to get me hired, despite any support from my network.

With this insane approach, I am constantly trying to assess my abilities as a person who can make great changes within companies by applying my knowledge and skills. My ME voice is telling me that I am not good enough, because who is going to hire a person who is faking it to make it?

I need to find something or someone to help me think differently so I can stop this crazy treadmill that I have put myself on. I go back to thinking that I need to re-evaluate the roles I envision myself being in, given my lack of self-esteem. I think that I need to start over again. I will go back to being a dutiful customer service representative, and rebuild my passion for business again. Only now, I am full of self-pity that I am going to be a loser in others' eyes for not continuing to pursue my passion for training and developing potential leaders. I want to scream out that I am a passionate person, who can make some great things happen, yet I can't stop the ME voice from telling me that I don't have what it takes to affect changes to enhance any organization.

At this point, you are probably wondering when this guy is going to have a nervous breakdown. Don't worry, so am I.

Luckily, I am praying for forgiveness and hoping that God will lead me to be rescued from myself. I am not preaching here, but I am grateful that my faith in God helped me to listen during the homilies rather than listen to my ME voice. I have always been a religious person, thanks to my mother's upbringing. Catholic guilt is what drives me sometimes. I feel guilty if I don't go to church. I feel guilty when I don't practice the Ten Commandments. Don't get me wrong; I have never murdered or stolen, or coveted my neighbour's wife (whatever that means to a gay man), but I have disrespected my mother, I have been jealous of my friends' possessions, and I have said the Lord's name in vain—all of which qualify!

I am not at peace with God, and that's why this is happening to me. Or at least that is what my ME voice is saying. That's the passion that is dying inside me, and the idea that one day I should just end it all because nobody will care. Wow, that is passionless self-talk at its finest.

My wandering thoughts are now leading me to do some self-reflection as to what I should do with the rest of my life. Today's social media makes it easy for you to find opportunities to start your own business. I have always admired my father, who ran his own business for forty years, because he was determined to make it on his own. I have the same perspective, because I have always prided myself as a strong decision maker and a trusted and reliable leader. Everyone tells me that there are great opportunities in coaching or consulting, and that my engaging behaviour is ideal, and I can fit right into the current fervour of marketing myself as a coach if I have a laser focus on what I can coach. Mind you, this is coming from people in the market for recruiting individuals to purchase memberships, materials, and programs to develop coaching skills so that you can market yourself as one.

I take on the role of coach but don't know what I can coach on!

I am researching different coaching skills to determine what kind of coaching would fit into my skill set. I think to myself that I can play the role of coach, and soon I will develop what focus I could market to gain clients. I start envisioning my future as a coach but still feel the need to stay within my comfort zone. I am combining all the expertise I have in call center management with the ability to coach others on their individual careers, since I am proud of individuals who have come back to me saying that they were inspired by me to take risks and work hard toward their career goals.

Goal setting is the key to success, as everyone knows. So, now I am setting my goal to be a coach who can help you through your periods of doubt and confusion. Meanwhile, I can't stay focused for more than ten minutes, but I know that once I get clients, all that will solve itself. This sounds ridiculous as I reflect on my thoughts, but I am convincing myself that this new plan, with clear goals, timelines, and my work ethic, will make this new role a reality. On to the next chapter, I say to myself every day, persuading everyone I speak with that I can coach with confidence and competence because I have been doing so throughout most of my career. The only problem is that I don't have any credibility because I have been marketing myself as a trainer, a learning and development consultant, a call center manager, and a director of operations, but never have I marketed myself as a coach. I hear that coaches are a dime a dozen or that everyone calls themselves a coach these days. Nonetheless, I am on this path because I have nothing to lose and everything to gain if this works out.

The only thing holding me back is me. Well, not really. My husband and life partner is starting to think that I am starting to lose it and that I should seek professional help. There is a history of mental illness in my family, and he's thinking that I am becoming a character from *One Flew Over the Cuckoo's Nest*. In all honesty, I am starting to act like Jack Nicholson, because my thoughts are erratically changing from wanting to find full time employment to trying to find the *right fit* in the current gig economy. Yes, that's something else I am learning about—the gig economy. The millennial generation who are the future of our society don't want to work 9 to 5 anymore. They want to work anytime of the day or night, and still be the favoured ones. My generation of putting in a full day in the office, being the go-to person for anyone needing assistance, doesn't mean much anymore. So, now I need to schedule time to speak with others as a coach or consultant and understand how to operate on their terms.

This doesn't work according to my need to be liked and appreciated. I am wondering how I am going to get the same satisfaction in thriving off other peoples' energies and input. I have worked actively with others to learn and develop my skills because I have always been a person who needs to be structured in the environment, where others feed each other ideas and recommendations to meet business goals and objectives. Where are the key performance indicators (KPIs) now?

I am lost in my sea of insanity, thinking that my calendar will be a substitute for my goal setting abilities. I structure my calendar to ensure that I am not letting each passing day go to waste. I want to be recognized for my organization skills so that I can convince myself that I can run my own business. My lack of discipline and concentration continues to haunt me because I can't keep the aggressive 8-hour day productivity tracking that I set out for myself. I feel defeated, and I abandon the idea of running my own business just as quickly as I decide on it. This means I am spiralling and spiralling out of control, leading me to feel useless and ineffective; until one day, I get a call from an insurance company for a role that I believed was my *right fit!* I know the company because a friend of mine has worked there for years, and I love the idea that their slogan is to *Make a Difference*. I know that they promote their business as a not-for-profit, so God is answering my prayers, and I will be employed again! I researched the company by reading articles, posts, and blogs about them. I heard from my friend that they need people with experience to solve their servicing problems, because they are experiencing long wait times to get through in their call center. They need strong leadership because they have experienced a lot of attrition, and they are developing their call center workforce by doing massive hiring to replace individuals

How to Love What You Think You Love

who have been there for some time. I know the industry and decided that I am the right person to fly in and set the plans, with lofty goals for which only I can execute. I am in control, and suddenly, I have a passion for life again! I am determined to land this full-time opportunity, and all my insane thoughts will diminish. I will be the saviour and the go-to person—that is my destiny!

Now, you must remember that I have been marketing myself and following every lead that is being offered me. I am hopeful that this time I will be rushed in to save the day, and all my worry, my unfocused energy drain, and my insanity will pay off. Then there's the waiting game.

That's the killer for me! My mind is racing with all the improvements, the meetings, and the collaboration that will earn me my VIP recognition award within my first three months. I have developed my first 90-day plan, which is what I have learnt is crucial to landing the *right* job these days. I am going to be the superstar the day I walk in, and that's what God has planned for me. Finally!

Well, I spoke with the talent acquisition person, who was very formal and listened carefully while I regaled her with all my past accomplishments. As well, she hears about how I have worked diligently to improve my skills so that I am ready and able to revise their current onboarding program. I have managed five direct reports in my last role as Manager of Training, Performance and Quality, so the requirement to manage five direct reports as trainers and curriculum designers is the *perfect fit*. She told me that I would be contacted to meet with the hiring manager within a few weeks, so I was convinced that they were

69

doing their due diligence and allowing others to apply for my role, to meet company hiring policy requirements. However, I didn't hear anything for about three weeks, and I was thinking to myself that my enthusiasm was not what they were looking for. At that time, I was informed that I would be meeting with the hiring manager to set up an interview. Meanwhile, I had already sent my resume and 90-day plan to the hiring manager because I was referred to him by my friend the previous week. I showed him that I had initiative, and that I was truly the right man for the job. This sense of pride and hubris comes naturally to me, so I know that I am on the right track. I have been searching to replace my last working conditions because I was very happy to be leading others while building out training modules, ongoing compliance training facilitated sessions, outlining learning objectives, and coaching others to be better versions of themselves. I had hit the jack pot!

Meanwhile, I was eager to prove that I had the goods, so I continued to read coaching books and training and facilitation text books so that I would be ready for the challenges to come. I was excited for my future and wanted to be the superstar, because I would be working and feeling productive. I needed to continue my daily ritual of working out and going to the library so that I could stay focused on meeting my goals of being prepared to lead a training team again. I am telling myself that I am proud of the discipline I am maintaining because I have set goals to stop hiding in my apartment. That's the learning that I can offer, that you need to find a way to be productive that allows you to focus on meeting your goals.

For a long time, I was making excuses for myself to combat my loneliness. One of those excuses was to have the television on so that I didn't feel alone when my husband was out working. The idea of hearing voices was to mimic the working environment, because I had always enjoyed the stimuli of other peoples' energies. I wanted to replicate the feeling of being in a busy office to avoid listening to my own thoughts. It's funny that I have always been afraid of being alone. I was a lonely child who didn't have many friends. I relied on television for companionship and did my homework in the living room to avoid feeling lonely. It wasn't until I was in high school that I focused my thoughts and concentrated on internalizing my studies, by working in my bedroom away from noise and distractions. Here I am again, in my fifties, and I am reverting to my childhood behaviours and wanting the comfort of the television to ease my pain of being unwanted. Unfortunately, I wasn't very productive because I would get distracted by the bombardment of talk shows, game shows, CNN updates, and home renovation shows. Now I was going to be a professional again, and work on myself at the library and gain the knowledge back that I felt I was losing. I wasn't going to go back into an office and feel that I couldn't operate without my daily fix of *The View*. Is any of this sounding familiar to you? If it is, then I recommend you find your own library because there are plenty of resources to occupy and help you concentrate to improve your perspective and understanding of your purpose in life.

That's what I thought I had found again: my purpose in life!

My purpose was to read anything that would suffice my thirst for knowledge about coaching, training, and facilitating at the public library. I had been studying for my exam for which I would be certified as a training and development specialist and enjoyed the feeling of being a student again. I wondered why I hadn't taken advantage of the space to focus my energies on improving my skills. I had to now forgive myself for thinking that watching TV was the cure for my pain. My mind was being stimulated, and I had people around who were like minded, even though I was older than most. I could even shelter myself from the homeless people who took refuge in comfortable chairs to sleep or simply hang out. This wasn't going to be permanent; I knew that I was going to get hired within the next few days.

Now I am seeking approval from myself that I am learning, reading, and applying my skills by working on plans to develop training programs without any actual programs. I review what this company does—that I have decided will hire me—and decide the type of coaching model that should be used to support the training transfer, based on my reading. I determine that the problems they are having as reported to me through my research will be solved once I sign the offer letter. This is fun!

A week goes by, and I hadn't heard back from the company. I started to panic and think that another month is going to pass, and I would still be unemployed. As luck would have it, I heard back from the talent recruiter, who told me that I had an interview set up with the hiring manager. *My email has worked! I am on my way to be a contributor in society again! I am going to be able to stop my thoughts of being broke and worthless and start planning for the coming interview.*

I was preparing my interview question responses, focusing on my client service management success stories, knowing that I would impress them with my expertise and knowledge. I used laser focus by highlighting times when I functioned well during crisis, and I knew that would be the deciding factor in their decisions. I had been waiting for this opportunity to demonstrate my management skills again, so I was excited to be considered for the role of managing others.

I went to the interview, confident that I would get the job. I felt like I was on the line from Chorus Line, singing again. *Oh God, I need this job. Please God, I need this job. I have to get this JOB!*

I was dazzling the hiring manager by asking questions about the current state of the call center. He shared with me that it has not been going very well. He said that he has been concerned about the amount of work and stress on the current employees, given the attrition they have experienced. They are doing constant hiring to replenish the existing complement, and need someone who can operate with a sense of urgency, to *skill up* the team. I assured him that I have been accustomed to ongoing changes within teams, and that I could help guide the current trainer to meeting the challenge. I was sharing my past experiences, when I was in a similar situation, and how I had implemented a buddy system to provide additional training to those who were fielding calls without receiving full training. I shared with him my experiences when I worked long hours to meet the increasing complaints being received, while training during peak working hours. I went on about my hands-on working style, thinking that would appeal to his sense of urgency, when he declared, "I know nothing about training." I answered his question when he asked what type of person I was, and I emphatically declared that I was a COACH, first and foremost. I was knocking it out of the park!

I left the interview, knowing that I had impressed him, as well as the other manager, who had been taking a copious number of notes as I turned on the charm. I felt like I had just given my sermon on the mount about the benefits of call center metrics, and how to use performance measurements to create learning objectives that would fast track training transfers. I promised that I could deliver the results he wanted, to improve the call center experience, as I would be on the management team. This was all going according to plan.

I didn't hear back for another week, but then I was called to schedule an interview with the senior manager of training and development, which excited my curiosity. *Are they planning on hiring me for a more senior position? Are they thrilled with my solution-oriented focus? Are they thinking that I need to validate my training skills? Do they want me to meet with the senior manager to get approval for the hire? What's going on?*

I was riddled with questions, but I remained calm. I went to the interview after reviewing my interview questions and responses, and I was determined to put on the charm again. After waiting for twenty minutes for the senior manager to arrive, I discovered that the hiring manager didn't know if I would be reporting to him or another manager functioning as a shared service within the operation. I thought to myself that this means that I would be working within Human Resources, if all works out, allowing me to expand my expertise. I was thrilled by the possibilities. I spoke with the senior manager, who confirms that I am who I say I am, based on some learning principle questions, the fact that I know what a learning management system does, and that I have previous experience working with learning designers, building online modules. It appeared that I had passed the test!

The following week, I got the verbal offer over the telephone, from the hiring manager, at which time we agreed that I would start in two weeks' time. I offered to start immediately, but he confessed that he was taking vacation and would not be prepared for me to start until he could arrange for my onboarding. I was keen to show my enthusiasm, and I offered to come into the office to meet with him so that I could see what the environment was like, and meet with some of his direct reports. I went to the office, two days later, and met with some of his direct reports to feel welcomed and appreciated for my people management skills. I met with the trainer, who informed me that the manager is a poor communicator because, if she knew they were looking for a team leader, she would have applied for the role. I heard about how the department is poorly managed because she had been training for the entire year without a break. I got a lot of complaining from her, and wondered how I could lead others by improving the management practices, as well as consult on how to improve performance objectives. I was thinking that they really needed me, because I received great feedback on my communication and management skills. I am the MAN!

I started the following week, to discover that the onboarding plan was for me to ask questions of one of the other team leaders who knows how the department operates. I dutifully sought to understand the working conditions for the team members that I would be leading. I was warned by my new direct reports that my enthusiasm for establishing the plan that I had provided, to make changes that would benefit the feelings of being unorganized chaos, wouldn't be accepted by the person who hired me. I am informed that the expectation to deliver great customer service wouldn't be accepted because the management doesn't want to bring in any more changes. My new training team members were under constant supervision by the current management team to take on work to support their interests rather than those of the team. I decided that I was in the wrong place and had made the wrong decision to accept the position.

What do I do now?

I continue to journal, with negative thoughts that I am not going to be able to work in the environment because I feel that it is too toxic. I write every day, thinking that I need to find another opportunity quickly or I am going to regret it. I participate in meetings, with a determination to improve the working conditions for the employees because I hear conversations that would never have been tolerated in a call center throughout my career. I walk in every day, like a soldier going to battle, to charge on with the armour that I have built, called my 90-day plan. I think that the reason I was hired is because I can influence a positive perspective on how to deliver customer service in a respectful and professional manner. I work on the centralized onboarding modules so that I can prove that I am a quick learner and that I can offer suggestions on how to introduce new staff in a structured and focused manner, only to find that I am not getting any kind of cooperation from the management team. I look around and see individuals in distress, and I have feelings of frustration and anger. The fact that employees are having awkward conversations because they are speaking with low class clientele, seems absurd to me. I have never been an environment where the customer is blamed for bad service experiences. I am shocked that existing representatives are permitted to condescend and belittle customers during inquiries, by over speaking and at times yelling to be heard on the telephone. I am biting my tongue when I see that the supervisors are sitting five feet away from individuals who are speaking with short, disinterested responses, for which no notice is taken. I am wondering how this culture can exist, when I have been in situations where arrogance and rudeness are considered performance infractions, and I am watching it be tolerated. I know that I won't be liked here because I am not hiding my feelings when I see that management is using band aid solutions and not getting to the root cause of the servicing issues. Wow was I a jerk!

I know now that I wasn't listening when others were telling me to SLOW DOWN. I was charging ahead, trying to prove my value as a qualified service professional rather than trying to understand the values that the management team was trying to encourage. I was using my energy to push my agenda rather than ask questions as to what the team management wanted to achieve, which was contrary to all that I had been studying for the last four months. I was on this bronco bull ride, and I didn't know how to turn it off!

I guess my reasoning then was that I was going to be a shaker and a mover, because I was introduced to everyone I met, with "Wow, you have a lot of experience and a great resume; we are looking forward to seeing what you can do". This confirmed that I was going to save the day by walking into the office every day, acting like SUPERMAN!

What am I going to do now? I am feeling like I am too old to start job hunting again. It had taken over nine months to land this opportunity, and I can't afford to go back on unemployment insurance because my debts keep increasing. I am in an anxious state and not able to sleep without awakening in a panic state in the middle of the night. I am drinking more coffee to keep my charge going, since I feel I must be the change that I am expecting of others. I am working through lunch, and arriving early and staying late, to prove that I can create the plan of action. I am reviewing materials to address the training needed to improve the customer service approach that will move the call center in the right direction. I am working with this sense of self-righteousness that I am going to take over the call center and ensure that the performance of the representatives will be held accountable. I am appalled to discover that the coaching model used only focuses on being nice to the customers, rather than defining what they do to have an impact on the customer experience. The service levels for completing requests is thirty to forty days, so I am confident that I can influence other processing teams to reduce the turnaround times to my previous five-day experience, by identifying root causes for delays. Meanwhile, I was hired to lead a five-person training team, with three members who have never formally coached others, a trainer who feels unappreciated by management, and a designer who is learning how to do the job. I have my work cut out for me!

I am working alone amongst a team of individuals who have worked together for some time. I am feeling underwhelmed by the responses that I get when I indicate how the plan to model the way through coaching sessions is received with trepidation. I wonder how I can make changes that will be positively received, because each day I sense more resistance and skepticism. I work with the lead supervisor to help her understand adult learning principles, while creating a job aid that was requested by the manager. I engage her to understand the outcome of using a job aid to manage callers by authenticating them thoroughly while employing privacy policy risk mitigation tactics. I meet with the privacy officer to confirm that the current policy requirements are being met, to avoid further customer conflicts, while validating identities. I am using my relationship management skills to ensure that the job aid will meet expected outcomes. I want to be seen as a leader, so I am providing guidance to her while she works to create the job aid to meet the manager's expectations. I believe that I am being effective, and that changes to improving customer interactions will begin by using the job aid for onboarding and ongoing call coaching purposes. Yeah! This is what they hired me for!

Well, that's what I keep telling myself! I must highlight my deep regulatory and compliance training to meet all the stakeholders' expectations. I am back, baby!

I am continuing to set goals because I have done so in my transition. I set goals such as meeting three new individuals a week to increase my network. I work on my goal of applying online for three positions weekly while engaging individuals within my network, who know the company culture, the role expectations, or the hiring manager, for positions for which I have applied. I schedule follow-ups for roles that I have applied for, on a weekly basis, depending on the closing dates of the opportunities. In most cases, I don't expend too much effort because job postings say that only those chosen for an interview will get replies. I lead and participate in an interview practicing group to seek feedback for my responses to possible interview questions. Also, I provide feedback to those doing the same so I can practice my coaching skills and provide insights, because of my extensive transition experience. This has been my full-time job, after all!

Now, I am faced with a REAL full-time job that isn't what I was expecting. I thought I could simply transfer my skills easily into an insurance company environment, with ease. I am realizing that the fast-paced wealth management operations within an insurance company doesn't deliver the same customer experience. How do I change gears and SLOW DOWN?

I was invited to meet with the assistant vice president, who I was introduced to during a meeting with all the operations leadership. I was asked to attend the meeting with my new manager, who has been working with me for about two weeks. I was thinking to myself that I must be doing some great work, as I walked into the meeting. However, I was told that my style was not being appreciated because I have been too aggressive in my approach: I have been seen rolling my eyes during team meetings; I have used profane language when speaking about staff; I have been over speaking others; I have been dominating meetings without understanding the expectations of the inter-action; and lastly, that I have no trust from my own five-member team. I was flabbergasted. I didn't understand how this could have happened. I had all the best intentions and yet couldn't see the impact that I was having on the organization. Now I wondered what was going to happen. I have never received such accusatory feedback before, because I have always been praised for my forward thinking, hardworking, and engaging management style. That was when my shame kicked in.

I was ashamed that I hadn't listened to my husband and best friend, who counseled me to listen more in meetings when I would tell them about what was happening. I was ashamed that I was not taking the time to seek to understand a guiding principle I had always used from Steven Covey's book, *Seven*

Habits of Highly Effective People. I was ashamed that I was being obnoxious and overbearing in meetings, when I had always prided myself as a great communicator. Lastly, I was afraid that I was going to lose this opportunity and be forced to tell people I had failed.

What do I do? I started reading veraciously again to see how I could quickly change this bad first impression. I spent the next two nights reading David Rock's *Quiet Leadership: Help People Think Better – Don't Tell Them What to Do: Six Steps to Transforming Performance at Work,* so that I could stop talking and start listening more. Now I am going to make a better impression so that they will have no choice but to like me!

You can imagine that I was burning the candle at both ends! I was still going in early, leaving late, and not taking lunches. I was going to make this work, despite that I didn't see myself working there for more than a year. I rationalized that I needed to change myself so that I could look for another opportunity, because everyone knows it's easier to find a job when you are employed. At least that's the myth that keeps playing in my head.

I was working with the guidance of my manager, who said she's glad to see that I realize that I need to change my management style, when I informed her of my plan to use the book exercises to hone my skills. I presented to her a plan for the upcoming professional development day, which was agreed by management, to skill up existing employees based on current performance gaps. I believed that my collaborative style would shine through because I had worked with my team to gather the materials and the agenda to present to her for her approval. I was back on track!

I continued to build the materials with my team over the next week, and things seemed to be progressing well. I was having fun creating a Jeopardy game-style interactive session to test product and process knowledge, with the assistance of the three individuals who would be presenting the workshop. I gave them ideas on how to organize and present the content so that we could get maximum participation and impact, and I incorporated participant evaluations so that we could take the feedback on how well the sessions were planned and executed so that they would serve to improve future training sessions. After all, I was under the impression that they hadn't done any formal training, by the reluctance they were communicating as we were constructing the content.

I thought to myself that we were working well as a team, and that I was gaining their trust.

The week before we were to deliver this fun, engaging and educating experience, I was released from the company. I was devastated, and I didn't understand why this was happening to me. I was doing what was asked of me: I was listening more; I was encouraging positive interactions with my team members; I was working on creating a great learning environment that was well received when we presented the plans to the management team members. Now what?

As I begged to understand why this was happening, I kept saying that all I was creating was structure that was lacking within the service center. I said to the Human Resources manager that there was tremendous employee dissatisfaction, and that other team leaders had told me that there were a lot of management problems in the service center. I was defeated! All the fight I was doing was futile. I was leaving. My days were going to be filled with shame, sadness, and sorrow once more.

This time, I was not going to be the loser. This time, I was going to show the world that I was right and they were wrong. This time, I was going to get the sweetest revenge, because they were going to call me back, saying that they had made a mistake and that I was the best thing to happen to that company.

Well, there was no call, and I am alone to bear the brunt of my failure. AGAIN!

Thankfully, my husband didn't divorce me. My family didn't abandon me, and my friends, with whom I shared my story, comforted me.

I needed to find a community so that I could find the courage to go on.

Luckily, I sought a mentor, whom I had known from my past life as a director of two of my greatest acting and musical production accomplishments. She has her own learning and development company, and agreed that I was the wrong fit for the environment. I was not to let this small blip ruin my career in the learning and development space. I was going to learn from my mistakes, and excel at my next opportunity. The only issue was ME.

I had to step back and reflect on how I was going to make changes in my life so that I could be a better person going forward.

That's when I had to stop the destructive behaviours that had taken control of me. I sought help from my physician and decided to quit smoking marijuana for good. It was doing me no good. I stopped drinking coffee to stimulate myself. I conditioned myself to drink socially on weekends so that I could still feel like I belonged within the circle of friends and family, without preaching about sobriety.

I wanted to be the ME I knew I had been in my younger years, without the pain of shame, depression, and anxiety that dictated my days. I had to make some personal life choices and seek help where I could. I have been reading a lot of self-help books that have served me to repair some broken relationships and bring love and laughter back into my life. I have practiced co-active coaching skills that I had learned from my studying for my Training and Development exam. I am proud to say that I am clearer now than I have been in years. Every day is a blessing, and I practice positive self talk and life affirmations that have stopped me from thinking I am unworthy and worthless.

I fill my calendar with promises to myself that I can keep, because I know that I will get ONE thing done each day, to lead a healthier and happier life. I am not going to allow a job to define me; rather, I will define the job I deserve.

> *"Without leaps of imagination, or dreaming, we lose the excitement of possibilities. Dreaming, after all,*
> *is a form of planning."*
> – Gloria Steinem

I love dreaming again! I dream about how I am succeeding at making relationships more robust, and how I can envision my future, sharing my pain so others can learn how to deal with theirs. I love listening actively and not allowing my internal dialogue to make me interrupt others. I love hearing about other peoples' perspectives and incorporating their learning into my life. I feel the intimacy of my relationship with my husband, which had been lost because of my anger, frustration, and bitterness. I am so blessed to have opened my eyes to the beauty of each day as the opportunity to live an abundant life of radiance and awe, as I have taken off the lens of shame. I must admit that it has taken courage, but the more I share my story with others, the more I see that vulnerability isn't a weakness but a strength.

I am not desperate to be employed; rather, I am eager to find the opportunity to use my skills without feeling ashamed of what will happen. I am excited to build my happy and healthy life around a career, rather than build a career around a miserable and anxious life.

When I was trapped in my shame of being unemployed, I couldn't speak openly to others about how I was feeling. Instead, I was worrying about what they were thinking about me being middle aged and being broke. Money comes and goes, but your character is with you forever. I am showing people my real character of being loving, open, honest, sincere, and wise. I know that there will be ups and downs as I continue to find ways to find my purpose, but I know how to re-purpose myself, based on listening while being present.

I dreaded each day having to explain why I hadn't found a job. Now, I don't worry about other people's perceptions. Well, I do care about what my husband, family, and close friends think of me. I know that their intentions and concerns for my sanity and my life are real. However, I don't have the need to justify myself anymore. Justifications are lies we tell others, which we think they will buy. They don't.

Gone are the days when I wouldn't allow myself to be happy because I was worried that others would judge me harshly for feeling blessed to be unemployed.

I have now been released from my pain and anxiety that I once thought motivated me to be liked and wanted. I learned that learning to like myself is more important than seeking to be liked by others. I say positive statements to myself, adding how and why I love the way my life is progressing. Feel free to use them yourself each day so that you can manage your ME voice.

These are the positive statements that I say aloud each day to get rid of my ME voice:

- Today is a GOOD day (I have been blessed.).
- I LOVE who I am (I am healthy, strong, and vibrant, and I have boundless energy.).
- I am GRATEFUL for this life (Happy marriage, loving family, great friends).
- I ACCEPT the things I cannot change. (The past is the past.).
- I don't KNOW everything (There are many skills waiting for me to learn.).
- Others don't DEFINE me (Others' perceptions are not mine.).
- LIFE goes ON (Ups and downs make life interesting.).

Chapter 6: How to Look and Feel Your Best for the Next 50

"I've been better served by aspiration… When I've been aspirational, I've focused on whom I might become."
– Jessica Hartogs

6

I am not 30 anymore, even if I think I am, is what I have been saying to myself to manage my expectations through this journey. As you know, to compete with others, you need to think like them. I have always believed this to be true. Any competition in life requires you to know your opponent. This is the fundamental understanding in races, sporting events, card games, board games . . . you name it. You need to know what your opponent is thinking so you can plan and anticipate your moves, how much preparation is required, and decide the amount of conditioning and training to beat them. Looking for your next job means that you must look like you know what is expected of you, to GET the opportunity. I have always prided myself in knowing that I must look the part whenever I have wanted to move within my career. The years of pursuing my acting career taught me that appearance and personality is everything, when you audition for parts in plays, movies, or commercials. I have been fortunate to apply that wisdom within my corporate experience, because I have had mentors who have subscribed to the same philosophy.

I was working for a wonderful mentor, who had inspired me to achieve my leadership role to gain his support to transfer from Toronto to Montreal, to lead administration and operations under his guidance. He was a well-dressed and articulate man who showed me that you are what you wear. Similarly, if you wear clothes well, people will be impressed with your taste in attire and how you carry yourself. I know that it is easy to think that appearance doesn't matter when you are submitting online applications and developing your network. However, the exact opposite is true, because the best way to find the hidden opportunities within organizations is to impress the individuals in the company where they work to help you get the job you want. I have always believed that people will easily recommend individuals who aren't going to damage or harm their reputation. Depending on the role and the culture of the organization for which you plan to work, allows you to adjust your wardrobe accordingly. These days, the corporate world has moved toward a business casual attire, whereby ties are archaic and old fashioned. However, if you aspire to management and leadership roles, you will want to appear that you are polished, well-groomed, and attractive to have those within the teams in the organization follow your direction. Luckily, age brings wisdom that people will automatically judge your abilities by first impressions. The drive to obtain interviews with hiring managers requires you to be ready, willing, and able to be seen at any time. I have found that you need to be healthy and happy in appearance, regardless of your emotional state. Career transition is like auditioning every time you meet with centers of influence who will recommend you as a qualified candidate, regardless of the role currently posted in the organization.

The difference between landing a job and going to interviews means that you can *fit the suit*. Every hiring manager has in mind the type of person that can *hit the ground running*. That means they will be well received and accepted as the *right* candidate as soon as they sign the offer letter. Let's face it, you must have the discipline to stay young looking if you are going to be competing for roles in which the hiring manager envisions younger, current, and adaptable individuals as the best candidates. The hiring process is usually in addition to all the other tasks and responsibilities that the hiring person is having to accomplish. It makes sense for them to pass judgements quickly, based on the social media society that we live in. Why would you not want to be considered for an opportunity because of poor grooming or an unhealthy appearance?

We live in a world where everyone makes judgements as to whether they wish to know more about you, within the first ten seconds. We are motivated by sight, smell, touch, taste, and sound. So, if you are networking to move into a targeted company for which you don't have a past connection, you need to manage your appearance to get the best chance to earn an interview. It's difficult to stay motivated when you are seeking a new job, because of the feelings of not having to be scheduled or expected to deliver results. Also, there are demons of self-doubt, apathy, and complacency that can appear, which may make you start acting in unhealthy ways. When I was working, I was always going to the gym, trying to eat well, and managing myself to take on challenges to prove my worth. Now, I don't have that momentum, so I need to stay healthy to be resilient and to face the rejection that is inevitable when looking for my next role.

The hunt for your next job requires you to be in consideration amongst the younger generation who may be savvier to social etiquette. I have found that technology has always been directed and accepted by the younger generation. I have been fooling myself thinking that being a Facebook user proved to everyone that I was current and knowledgeable about what it means to live in the 21ˢᵗ century. Technology has been moving at such a pace that language, science, and business requires you to be aware of how to conduct yourself to meet the "show me why we should hire you" mindset. Furthermore, we need to put the elephant on the table and declare that ageism exists wherever you go. There is something to be said for not being a risk to companies because of poor choices, since you will need to prove your worth time and again.

For me, that desire to prove myself has come from vanity. I have always been vain since I learned as an overweight child how cruel people's comments can be. I remember how I was teased and mocked by being the last one picked when deciding teams on the playground. I remember when people would comment if I was eating too much. I remember when I was called names and laughed at for being the fat kid. I remember when I was not asked to hang out with others because I was told that I would embarrass them. All these cruel taunts still exist today. However, they are done with a sense of shame that you aren't good enough to be considered acceptable to others within their circles.

Now, you might be thinking that comparing your networking efforts with the taunts and behaviours of children is unfair or unrealistic. However, people's attitudes remain the same when they are concerned with other people's perceptions of them. Besides, aging itself causes people to be fearful that they will take on people management issues if you don't fit into their current working teams, which are comprised of individuals who have just entered the workforce or in the prime of their working years.

I have never experienced ageism directly but often hear about it from people who were working to find the *right* candidates to meet their hiring needs. It's funny because the fear of 50 occurred when I was leading a team of predominantly women, in Montreal. There was a situation with a supervisor, who was a fashionable dresser, outspoken, and articulate. When I realized that she was causing dissention among the teams because she was very vocal in her opinions of the appearance and conduct of others, I had to question her ethics. She was turning 50 and was fearful of losing her position, and she expressed that it would be difficult for her as a woman to find another job quickly, because people would judge her by her age. She decided that she would find another job before she would be released, so that she had the upper hand in the manner that she might leave the company. It struck me then, as I was in my mid-forties, that age is the *silent killer* when it comes to people's egos and self-esteem.

What ever happened to respecting your elders? The western civilization tends to view elders as slower, inflexible, intolerant, and ineffective. Meanwhile, the pace of change in businesses has created knowledge drains as people are being forced to leave organizations and are taking all their knowledge and experience with them. There has been a war on talent that I have come to hear about in the corporate world for most of my career. Well, now the guns are pointing at me, and simply because I have been around too long.

It's strange that I am expounding on the societal changes, where youth and vibrancy are traded off for maturity and experience. I have been working in the training and development space, within operations of insurance companies, for over the last five years. I have noticed that a reliance on just-in-time training, and ongoing skill development to meet immediate business needs, seems to be prevalent as companies compete in the global economy. It isn't about how much you know but what you know you can learn and adopt quickly that determines your success to meet ongoing changing circumstances. There is a sense of urgency to find individuals who have education achievements, rather than working experience, to meet innovation and digital environment management needs.

While in transition, you are expected to be viable and current within your industry, your profession, and your perspectives. The old expression, *birds of a feather flock together*, comes to mind whenever I hear people feeling slighted by the thought of not getting interviews because they don't have the educational requirements that are being recruited. I have been down the same negative path, believing that I am not qualified to apply for roles that I am well suited for, because my experience doesn't mean that I can put letters behind my name.

My goal is to be healthy and attractive, with my best smile, to gain contacts while networking. I know that discipline distinguishes people, when speaking about my daily regimen of vigorous cardio exercise combined with weight training to maintain a young appearance. I am lucky that I come from a line of people that have looked younger than they are, so the gene pool is helping me to compete. Also, the fact that I want to stay healthy to avoid illness and injury makes me feel blessed when I see others who haven't been as diligent. I suggest that you assess your own unhealthy habits and use the time you have in transition to make healthier lifestyle choices. I believe that owning your choices to be healthier at this stage of life provides you the inner strength and self-confidence that time isn't against you. Instead of wondering what the future holds, making positive life choices in the present serves to build better habits once you land a job that places time demands on you. Besides, wouldn't you want to fool future employers and fellow employees that you are younger than you really are? Your chances of adjusting to new working conditions will be easier if you are *the bird who can flock together faster*.

It helps to surround yourself with younger people who can make recommendations of how to be youthful. Also, I have learned so much from being active and social with younger individuals within my community theatre and networking groups. I have discovered that there are many ways to remain vibrant and current by asking how to use technology to optimize productivity. There is so much to learn when you are seeking your next purpose in life. The feeling can be overwhelming!

I have always used technology to stay involved when I was employed. It gets to be a mental acuity challenge to know which social platforms are preferred to use, versus the ones to avoid. The different methods of using technology require practice and patience to use them for maximum impact. I have considered myself to be a lifelong learner, because you stay younger by learning something new every day.

Now, as the year has progressed, I know that my fear of technology was limiting me to the joy of discovery, because I lacked patience with myself. I wanted to use the same applications because I didn't want to go out of my comfort zone. I have now set goals for myself to learn one new functionality on my cell phone and computer each day, so I can leverage the fast pace of technology as my way of staying current. It seems the days of identifying myself as a FAST follower have slowed down to a SLOW crawler.

I was allowing myself to lack control of my negative thoughts. The realization that a positive body image focus to look skinnier still requires a healthy spirit, has done wonders for my self-esteem. The way we speak to ourselves during this search for purpose again, requires the cup-half-full approach. I guess getting older means you become the cup-half-empty in your thoughts. Well, I must admit that I was always thinking less of myself than I should have, because I have had some great accomplishments in my life thus far. However, by allowing substance abuse to manage my moods and my spirit, it was destroying my self-esteem and self-confidence.

I find that searching for your next chapter means understanding how you will re-purpose yourself so that others see you as forward thinking and future focused. It can be contrary to how you feel as you delight in and explain all your past accomplishments. Why not start to make nutritional choices that you can share with others, as examples of how you self-manage in organizations that value wellness in mind, body, and spirit?

I have been learning the value of discipline and dedication to accomplishing goals that are for me, and not for the business that I am leading. You recall that I was moving through life accomplishing key performance objectives that I identified as goals. I translated the goals I had in my work life as personal goals because I was seeking to move up the corporate ladder. My ability to use effective goal setting measures has restored my self-esteem and self-confidence. That is something that you must continue to guard as you go through your journey to find your next purpose. I had linked my purpose to my job and my role within the company I was employed. I had always told myself that there is more to accomplishing professional goals; but, deep down, I never really documented any progress of my personal goals. I recognize the value of writing down your goals and reviewing them on a frequent basis. I believe that you need some time to allow yourself to make your goals a reality by what you complete daily. So, now I am detailing my progress on a monthly basis to ensure that I am on track with the timelines I have set for myself. It's funny that it has taken this time of searching for my next chapter, for me to come to appreciate the spirit of documenting my life's story by the goals I am accomplishing.

When I hear the word, *discipline*, I think of school-aged children who are told what to do. I am now understanding that the same is true for when you are entering this new world, attempting to re-purpose yourself. When you are working at the same company for some time, you know that you are being told what to do by the environment in which you are working. You know that you need to be on time to work. You know that you must prepare yourself for meeting the day's challenges, meetings, calls, and presentations. You know that you must be planning while evaluating what has been done, so you know what your priorities are to be achieved. You know that you must achieve. You know that you must be thinking about the changes within your industry or profession for which you need to manage. All of this requires you to be disciplined. Then, when you are no longer a part of that organization, you may lose your ability to be disciplined, because there isn't the office or the group of individuals relying on you to perform. For me, the power of commitment and dedication to improve the working environment has always been my motivation. Now, with no working environment or team of people relying on me, what's my motivation?

Here I am, working to be wanted and needed again, by disciplining myself to work on my skills to improve my chance of contributing to the companies where I want to work. I have been using online tutorials to build my skills, but my problem is that I still don't feel needed. I need to refocus myself to not work with imposed project deadlines or business initiatives that are scheduled out for me. I must find the inner strength to improve my skills so that when the time comes, I am calm, cool, and collected. The mind is willing, but the heart isn't. I don't have the heart to enhance and build my skills if nobody cares. I have been telling others that I am working on myself rather than authoring tools to build out modules that nobody will use. My spirit isn't connecting to my current reality of working alone. I am ashamed of myself for not keeping up my skills, and I wonder when I will have the chance to use them again. The goals are easy to write down; it's doing them that becomes difficult when you are in the company of one.

I have always enjoyed learning new things, and now I am not anymore. The fun isn't there anymore until I can find some fun in my days. It becomes an inner battle with myself as to what is more important: spending time with friends, family, or myself, rather than improving my network contacts or sharpening my skills. I can tell you that you carry tremendous guilt if you think about taking the day OFF. In my past life, I would never take days off unless I was very sick. Even then, I would go to work, because the priorities to finish tasks to meet commitments outweighed the need to take care of myself. I had people telling me to go home when I was congested, coughing, and exhausted with the common cold, because I felt guilty calling in sick. The idea of working from home has always been a misnomer for me because I was conditioned to believe that your home wasn't your workplace. Your home was your sanctuary from work, because it represented a place to relax and release the pressure to be "on." I guess that's what led to my substance abuse problems: because I didn't know how to relax. I have always had to have multiple balls in the air to feel liked and wanted. Now, I have no balls (figuratively speaking), and I am wondering how I can get some balls back!

As a person at the end of the Baby Boomer generation, and at the beginning of the Generation X generation, it is necessary that I clarify that I have always felt I needed to be a part of a greater cause. The need to be a 9 to 5er still continues to be my Achilles heel. I grew up watching my mother and father working Monday to Friday to make the best of their livelihood for us. I watched as my father would leave home by 7:30 AM so that he could open his car repair business at 8:00 AM, to allow customers to drop off their cars before going to their jobs by 9:00 AM. I still feel guilty if I am not working by 9:00 AM now, even though there isn't any logical reason for me to be so. I appreciate that the generations that are working now can work anywhere and anytime. I just don't know how to conform to the norm that work isn't accomplished without being in the place where others are doing the same thing within the same timeframe. Our global economy has erased the concept of thinking of being in your own time zone to work.

Now you ask, what rock have you been living under?

Yes, I know that this may sound old-fashioned, but I like going to work! I like socializing with colleagues. I like being seen working to accomplish my professional goals! I like knowing that others are dependent upon me to show up and do my best, and to finish my day thinking that I am moving the business forward.

The coming generations are going to experience the feeling of working much differently than I or you have.

They will likely be the next wave of workplace practices to have more fun at work instead of making work fun. They will want to work within teams to accomplish goals to better the industry with which they work, rather than be concerned about market share within the industry. They will work to make society more inclusive rather than finding a means to be considered exclusive when managing daily tasks. They will be the generation to work on a twenty-four-hour clock, rather than punching a clock. They will communicate anytime, using social platforms to move business forward, to change how they do business rather than waiting for the business to change. They will look to individuals to use their strengths in unison, rather than singling out an individual's strengths. Lastly, they will not need to hear about "do you remember back in the day," because their days are filled with what is important and occurring now.

This is the new world in which I am re-purposing myself, so that in some way, I can be respected for my talents rather than for my experience.

Wow, what a different way of thinking.

I have always been influenced by television as my means of

validating how life should be. Now, it's time to turn off the TV, because the generations that will be industry leaders don't watch it. I am charging ahead, using Instagram, Twitter, Facebook, Reddit, and whatever other application I hear about from younger people, which will serve me to stay in the know.

What a change of pace we are currently experiencing. The world has become a constant filtering of what is fake and what is real. How can I adapt to making an impact when I don't know what or who can be impacted?

Welcome to the world where youth is applauded and maturity is questioned.

I guess you now think I am a SUPERHERO who can leap tall buildings at a single bound. I am running around with this renewed energy and purpose, trying to save all *job loss survivors.* Well, in a way, I am. It's the choices you make every day that define your hero to yourself. I may seem like I have it together all the time, but I am still ME. That voice reappears when I don't expect it. But the beauty of my life now is that I know what triggers it. I know that when I get envious or jealous of others' successes, I am being the OLD ME—the one who was self-pitying and resentful, and playing the victim— because I was feeling that this was punishment for something that I was doing wrong.

> *"There is beauty and humility in imperfection."*
> – Guillermo Del Toro

Life is full of choice, so I choose not to be the person I was hating during my search to settle for anything that comes along. I am choosing to be the best person who listens, cares, and understands that life is a journey and not a life sentence. I am including a picture of what I believe everyone searching for their purpose must understand. Every day matters, and what you do today will impact tomorrow. Remember that it has taken the choices you have made over the last five decades to get where you are today. Life has a destiny, and it is available for you to know what that is if you have the courage to master your talents, your strengths, and your character to make changes to meet your next challenge. This is what a real SUPERHERO is all about in these days of extreme changes in the workplace, the family, and the world, as we continue to embrace technology and the digital age; and all that we can do is go along for the ride.

I am blessed to have some amazing people take the ride of self-discovery and self-awareness as they are on their path of care. I have been able to see that your ability to manage the ups and downs of hope and despair builds inner strength that no job or place of employment can ever give you. It's amazing for me to see the glimmer of hope in your eyes when you tell me that you may be landing your next dream job. I am mesmerized by you when you show me that you are starting the following week and can't wait to join humanity again. I am astonished when you walk with pride after getting your second or third interview, for a role in a company that you admire and hope to build your career in again. Also, I am saddened when you aren't chosen for the role, or didn't get a second interview, or got a rejection letter. I am saddened because you must realize that it wasn't the right place for you anyway.

Faith in yourself, but also faith in a higher power, allows you to enjoy the wins during career transition, but more importantly, to learn from the losses. I know that getting interviews are blessings that are provided me to hone my skills and my self-confidence, and to demonstrate my talents. I want you to think the same, because you don't have a crystal ball to let you know when you are getting your next offer. Just know that you will, if you stay focused, level headed, healthy, and strong. So, the negative thoughts may come, but it is managing them that makes you a SUPERHERO to yourself.

I celebrate my successes no matter how small they may appear to someone younger than myself. I am no longer having to compete with someone half my age to feel worthy. I am powerful, charming, and wise for my years, and that's what people will see and feel when meeting me for the next 50 years! When you celebrate your daily wins, your next chapter is unfolding before your very eyes. You just have to open your eyes to see it!

Now that you have seen my journey to finding my purpose, I had the blessing of other members of a very important group in my life. I realize that the more I share my journey, the more my thoughts and anxieties are felt in others. The next chapter is an opportunity for you to see that you are not alone in managing guilt and shame while going through job loss and transition.

Chapter 7: When to Help Others
(It's Our Journey)

"You make a living by what you get;
you make a life by what you give."
– Winston Churchill

7

I have been lucky to have been blessed with great people in my life to guide me throughout my career. When I wasn't working with them, I had lost touch because of the pain that I was feeling, of not being wanted by them. I have come to realize that the circumstances that were occurring at the time were what I needed in order to forgive myself. I was avoiding them to avoid the pain of losing the future I had envisioned with working alongside them at that time in my life. This journey of career transition had taught me that I don't need to blame anybody for not being a part of the corporate organizations that I was fortunate to experience. Also, I have come to appreciate that others who are going through career transitions, experience similar feelings of loss, like the five stages of death. I know that job loss is one of the most stressful experiences, next to the death of a loved one, from my days of studying behavioral psychology. Now, I am recognizing in myself and others the impacts it has on your character and your perspective on life. Through my weekly sharing of individual experiences, from members of a networking group in which I belong, I have been seeing the effects of going through anger, denial, bargaining, self-pity, and acceptance of the loss that I have experienced. I have always been a person to give myself wholeheartedly to my role within teams; so, when I was no longer a part of the team, my world and my heart felt emptied.

In writing this book, I had decided to have the courage to share my thoughts, feelings, my fears, and my depression, so that you could learn from it. Similarly, I am privileged to have had interviews with members of my networking group, to understand their perspective of their career transition journey. I have come to realize that sharing the ups and downs of seeking your next chapter allows you to speak about your emotional and spiritual experiences that help and hinder your ability to *get over it.*

I am providing you with the questions and responses as I interviewed three amazing women who offered to share their stories. I will not be identifying them by name for privacy reasons, but I hope that you will be able to see that we are all human, and we all face daily challenges to preserve ourselves to be ready for what comes next.

The next portion of this book is written in a question and answer format for ease of understanding, and for consistency in understanding, that you are not alone.

Did you think that you would be on this journey at this point in your life?

The first woman expressed how she was at a point in her life where she was comfortable dealing with the emotional ups and downs of career transition, because she knows what her priorities are in her life. She said, "I never had a journey in mind. I am one of those people who say, 'I don't know what I want to be when I grow up.' I have been in program and project management for more than 15 years, and this in my third layoff in my career, so I am OK with it. The first one was scary, but the second one was not as scary because I was in the United States at the time. The only reason I could be there was because of my work VISA. As soon as that VISA expired, I had 24 to 48 hours to leave. That was scary because I had my whole life there, including my apartment to deal with. Here I am at my third layoff, and I am going back to program and project management, partly because of financial responsibility. I have a plan to retire at 55. Retirement for me means not having to depend on a specific level of income. It doesn't mean I would stop working, but I would have to do something; otherwise, I would be extremely bored. If I could retire at 55, I would be OK with starting all over again. But now, I am not willing to start all over again. Program and project management is not my passion. At this point in my life, I am not willing to start all over again.

My career was the big thing for me, but it has become less so now. As I climbed the corporate ladder, I realized that the higher I went, the more politics I would have to deal with. I decided that I didn't want to seek that anymore. Job satisfaction is still important to me. What I am realizing now is the importance of work/life balance. I was hungrier when I was younger, but I have started to figure out what is good enough for the person I am now. I am not going to perfect the presentation that I am working on. I will still do my best, but it may take me five instead of ten hours to create it. I am still proud of the work I produce, but it has taken time for me to realize what is *good enough*.

You see, my sister passed away, and I helped take care of her and her two children while she was sick. I was lucky I had an understanding manager who allowed me to do that because I could be relied on to produce quality work. He would comment that I would return work assigned within 12 hours, when sent it on a Friday night. Now that my sister has passed, I pick up my nephews from school, two to three days a week. So, my priority is to be available to them because my nephews are at such a young age, they need me. I know, as they grow, they may not need the extra attention I am giving them now, but I am glad to support my brother-in-law as a single parent. I never thought I wanted children, so I never thought I would be helping to raise them. I know what my priorities are now."

The second woman had more of a plan that she would be working, and now she is dealing with the reality that she's not. She was in shock, realizing that this was not what she had planned. She expressed, "I thought I would be working until I retired, at the same organization, because I worked hard and took my vacation each year, and my life was set. The wheel that I was chugging along on suddenly stopped. I was startled by being thrown out. The rug was pulled out from under me. I wake up and I'm not the same person anymore. It's hard to reflect that my life isn't going as planned. I have to look at my family and finances, but my husband and I get into disagreements. Before, finances were never a concern; now, we have arguments about income coming in to support our children. I am less patient with my kids, because I want them to start earning income for themselves so I don't have to worry about them. I have become a horrible person sometimes. I have my family telling me what I should do. They are all concerned for me, while they keep telling me I should be able to find a job. They want to help me because they see the struggle I am going through. I get angry because I need to deal with this alone. I like being independent, but sometimes it becomes overwhelming. This networking group allows me to talk about it without feeling judgement. As time passes, I start to feel that I am not qualified anymore, even though I exceled in my last role without a designation. Now, I need to get a designation to prove what I did for years. Now, they can hire someone at half my salary and my age. I may have to settle for half of what I was earning, and it hurts. I sometimes feel that I don't want to apply for roles for that reason. I am learning how to deal with my feelings, and I am OK with learning how to improve my interviewing skills."

The third woman, who shared her response to my journey question, brought to light how her faith in God helps her. This, I found to be profound, because I am a firm believer that there is a reason for everything, and every challenge in life provides great appreciation for having a predetermined destiny.

She started explaining that she had a great career, as she was promoted several times over a few years, for the company where she worked. She wasn't expecting to be released. She said there was a change in management, which changed the strategic plans, meaning there were too many people when the new structure was announced. She was pleased that they communicated the changes, allowing her to seek other roles within the organization. She was offered other jobs that didn't align with her career goals. She wasn't going to settle for something that would not advance her career. She had three months to find another opportunity within the company, while she could look externally as well. During that time, she didn't look externally, hoping that she would find the right opportunity within the company that she enjoyed being in. In the end, she decided that she would leave to find another opportunity, by updating her resume and enhancing her job search skills. There wasn't anything keeping her at the company. She was grateful that she had time to process the anger and self-pity that she was a top performer. She wanted to leave without any bitterness.

She was relieved when the day came to be released, because she saw that other people were not acknowledging the change in the company culture. She saw others floating around, not speaking about it, and realized that she needed to leave for her well-being. She felt the departure was easy by making the decision makers feel comfortable. She said, "I made sure not to burn any bridges. I wanted to make sure that I was not taking this personally. My Christian faith allowed me to ensure that I was going to be better for leaving, because I received my confirmation by addressing my fear of leaving. I prayed and felt that I had more to learn by leaving than by trying to stay. My clarity was in trusting God that there was something better waiting for me. I needed to hold his hand and trust that he would lead me through this new world that I didn't know about. It was easier to let go, knowing that God was steering my path. It was then that I passed the stage of questioning why this was happening to me. My last day, I sent notes to all those that I worked with, thanking them for the great opportunities I had, and by doing so, they wanted to stay connected. That helped me to feel that I was going to be OK when I left. "

I appreciate that these three individuals were at different stages of their journey. One was recognizing that her family value was her priority, giving her meaning as to how she was learning to accept another layoff, having faced the challenge before. The second was still dealing with being angry that her life plans had changed, and she needed a safe place to deal with her thoughts and feelings, while the last one was in denial for a time, until she relied on her faith to move past the bargaining stage, to realize that she was ready to learn how to excel again in different ways.

This was very powerful for me, because I saw in each of them how I had used the opportunity of sharing my thoughts in the same environment of our networking group, over the last 12 months, to continue to heal myself.

How do you stay motivated and focused during your career transition?

This question was interpreted in different ways because each of the respondents had to convey their shame and guilt in how they approached the process of job searching. I have felt the same in looking how to focus and target what I want to do each day when faced with multiple stimuli from job search tools and networking, and coping with the highs and lows on my emotional roller coaster.

The first woman I interviewed talked about the language she speaks to herself, which can demotivate her at times. She said, "I have a lot of thoughts about what I should be doing and what I will do, but I will be honest; I am not really motivated. I have a list of all the things that I should and can be doing, and I do some of them but not all. I set a daily goal of doing three things, and end up doing one. Sometimes I don't do any of them because I got a good package. I don't have any financial pressure because I am single and have saved my money. I like to say that I am being selective in what I want to apply for. There are days when I am motivated, and I will get those three things done because I feel accountable to our networking group when we meet weekly. I get motivated by hearing another individual's momentum. I get excited about the search again. I know I just have to get started, because I dislike networking. I purchased a ticket to attend a networking function, with like-minded individuals in my industry, to show the group that I am out there networking. My days are somehow filled because I am enjoying my sabbatical. It makes me wonder how I got everything done that I wanted to do when I was working. It is just a matter of focus and personal satisfaction."

The second woman I interviewed spoke about how she stays focused in her life as well as during career transition. She wanted me to understand that she defines her daily priorities based on her family values and desire to be appreciated for efforts that she takes to make her family's life better, rather than just focus on her job search. She said, "I decide each day how to prioritize my energy because there is so much information that comes at me each day. I could be learning new software, working towards my industry designation, and trying to meet new people to expand my network. At the end of the day, I need to reconcile with myself how much I am going to increase my value by doing all those things but not spending time and attention on my family. I know I have the skills to re-enter the job market, and I am looking at settling for a role that can be an opportunity to get into an organization. However, I know I may be settling for less money and a more junior role. I feel rejected because I bring value beyond the amount of my salary. I know I am not the only person thinking this way, because I have spoken with other people who have the same skills and can't find employment. We have lost humanity somehow, when employers are seeking to find the best talent at the cheapest price. When I started working at the bank, I was one of the youngest in my department, and when I left, I was one of the oldest. It's hard because, in my mind, I don't see myself as an older person. I don't see myself as being old, even though I may cover the grey. People look at you, and they judge you by trying to figure out how old you are. I am 56 years old, and people always say that I look younger. When I was younger, that seemed old, but I don't feel old. So, it is hard staying focused to get back into the workforce."

The third woman revealed that it was a struggle between herself and God, because the daily momentum felt uncomfortable by relying on Him to guide her to the right opportunity. She indicated that if she goes anywhere where He doesn't want her to go, she will not have his favor. She was very honest in saying, "I am waiting on Him to give me instructions on what to do. He placed me on this path, and he blessed me with the promotions and salary increases that I received at the company where I was for most of my career. I know that if He doesn't provide the opportunity, then I won't have the same favor. I am seeking Him to discover where He wants me to go next." I say to Him, "If you asked me to leave my current company, where do you want me to go next? It has not been clear, even though I have had offers over the last few months. I treated them as demotions, so I decided not to accept them. I have had rejections for the roles that I felt in my heart were the right ones. I have been distracted and unmotivated recently as I look through job postings. I try each morning to connect with Him to decide how much time to spend on looking through job postings. I pray all the time for his guidance. I received a rejection for a role that I recently applied for. He helps me to know that it wasn't meant for me. I ask for wisdom for what to do. I get the impression of what to do, the same way as how I know how to help people that I encounter. I pray and ask God how I can help this person. When we meet weekly, I ask God what He wants me to tell them, and what they need to practice, when listening to other's updates. I stay motivated by listening for God's wisdom, because

I believe He knows more than I do about my purpose."

All three of these women demonstrated their courage and love for themselves and others, which continues to be the motivation to live healthier and happier lives. I was extremely moved by their honesty, as I came to realize that they all inspired me to think of the journey of career transition as an opportunity to reflect on the power of selflessness, rather than selfishness, when promoting myself to find purpose again.

How do you feel in the morning about continuing the journey of career transition?

The first woman got into the way she looks at her schedule in the morning to plan out her day, to determine what the day going forward would be like. She reinforced her need for work/life balance to be her priority. She indicated that she needs to schedule time to pick up her nephews from school, because that is important to her. She gave me an example of a recent interviewing experience. She accepted a second interview for the Monday following her initial interview, on the previous Thursday. The interview took three and a half hours, meeting with the vice presidents, in the targeted company. She asked about the culture, concerning the flexibility of hours in the office. She informed the hiring manager that she would need to leave at 4:00 PM to pick up her nephews from school. The hiring manager responded by telling her that would not be acceptable because it would mean that her absence would need to be covered by someone else. She indicated that she would be available any time remotely, should the need arise. Unfortunately, that would not work within that company, and she decided not to pursue the opportunity any further. This showed that she knows what she is willing to settle for in finding the right fit, as well as opportunity.

The second woman goes with the flow. She plans what she wants to accomplish for the day. There are days when she wants to be productive, and there are days when she doesn't want to do anything. She said, "On days when I have slept well, I get up and get things done. Some days I have more energy than others. Right now, I am not sleeping well. I find I don't sleep as much as I used to because I don't exhaust myself as much as I did when I was working. Now I have the flexibility of sleeping in or staying up late. I read or binge watch TV, which is terrible because I also snack at night, and I know it isn't healthy for me. Sometimes I feel like I don't have any purpose. I feel lost because I am too young to retire, and I hate it when I hear that I should retire. When I retire is not up to anyone but myself. I have lots of ideas and skills that I am not using right now."

The third woman was very real and authentic in discussing how she feels about facing the day, and not needing to dress professionally. That was very compelling because they say you are what you wear. So, I probed to hear how she faces her day. She explained, "When I was in the bank, I had to dress formally. Now I am wearing jeans because I don't have anywhere to go. I feel different. I feel like I am an outcast. I felt less but I went back to my faith. I need to understand who I really am. I am still valuable and important because I am more than just what I am wearing. I am not someone who is defined by a 9 to 5 job. I am not defined by what I wear. I am not defined by how I look. I am a daughter of the King of Heaven. I refocused my thoughts on my identity, which is based in Christ. If I based myself on fleeting things like wealth and social status, I would easily crumble when they are gone. When I reframed my thoughts, I wasn't full of self-pity because I don't wear power suits now or am not part of the crowd, rushing to be somewhere. When I reframed my thoughts, my emotions followed. When I start thinking about what I don't have, I am going away from Him, and that's when the trouble comes. Trouble is always there when you are distracted. I went through the anxiousness when I questioned God's purpose for me. I had moments of self-doubt. I relied on other Christians to pray for me and with me, to help me remember why faith is so important to me. We want to understand what's going on. It's been hard for me to trust Him, but I know that when I do, I can face the day."

These revelations show that you can draw from your own experience, your own faith, and your own beliefs in a higher power, as well as from your values and your character, to find your purpose, without having to have a job to define you.

How do you cope with the isolation of being on your career transition journey?

I believe that we, as humans, seek for affiliation, association, and belonging, much like being in a tribe. The hardest part of the career transition journey is feeling isolated and alone, because there isn't a constant of individuals who are working together to accomplish common goals. I have always been very motivated, knowing that my daily efforts were having an impact on others while contributing to mutual success. I posed the question of coping with isolation because I have found that networking creates a feeling of trying to belong somewhere.

The first woman indicated that she didn't feel isolated because the working environment that she had left was toxic. She felt that it was a positive change by moving away from that tribe. She went on to explain, "There are multiple tribes available to me. There's the tribe of jobs, friends, running, spinning, and family. The only thing missing from not having a job tribe right now, is not having someone to talk to everyday. I must admit, when I see my friend at spinning every week, I hear, 'So, how is the job search going?' I am tired of the question, because of the judgement that comes along with it. I choose the words to respond by saying I am enjoying my sabbatical. I had been working at one company for 16 years, which doesn't reflect my entire career. I would like some time off for me. I haven't done a whole make-over, but I am getting some stuff accomplished around the house.

While I don't feel isolated, I do have the feeling of rejection, from the multiple times I haven't heard back from companies after applying. I did do the right things by customizing my cover letter, and I ensured that I had the key words in my resume to match the job description. I was glad that they rejected my application on one hand, but it was disheartening because I put quite a bit of effort into modifying my resume and customizing my cover letter for that job. Then I was told, *YOU are not good ENOUGH.* I was hurt personally. So much for what my parents would say— that I get an A for effort. All that work didn't matter. Statistically speaking, I have to be prepared mentally for the rejection. Just because they don't respond, or I am rejected, or I make it to the third interview, I still might not be the right candidate. My goal is to get the interview to practice my interview skills, if nothing else."

The second woman interpreted the question as feeling that she doesn't identify with isolation, because she reaches out to people, which helps her to not feel alone. She said, "I have friends and family. For example, my dad is an amazing man. My dad can talk to me for hours. My mom is another story. All I hear from her is her complaining about my dad, or about her pain. But my father is always there for me. I also have my younger sister, who pushes me to do things, and she means well. She is my reality check if I am overeating because I am stressed. She questions if I want to be fat and unhealthy. My other sister is very wealthy and spends money on me as her way of showing she cares about me. She takes me out for dinner because she thinks I need money. I don't need money; I need someone to spend time and understand what I am going through. She has never been through this, so she doesn't know what it's like. I am never isolated, because there are people in my life who care about me."

The third woman indicated the importance of getting out of the house and to have the purpose of finding a job in order to belong again. She indicated that she gets demotivated when she is at home. She wants to get out and speak with others to find motivation and not feel isolated. She has two networking groups because, by helping others, it helps her to stay on track with what she needs to do. She told me, "I am travelling a lot for social obligations, to feel a part of something." She went on to say that by speaking with others, she becomes accountable, because she mentions what her plan is for the day. She also went on to say, "I go to the gym, and he asks what the plan for the day is, so I don't want to feel guilty if I don't do what I say I am going to do."

Each of these open and honest women appeared to me to be having internal struggles, to reconcile not being in a *tribe*. However, each them recognized the value of human kindness, and sought out opportunities to belong in order to avoid the feelings of being unwanted. That was inspirational for me, because the secret to finding your purpose again is finding where you want to belong, by who you associate with.

What is your relationship with time at this point in your journey?

Time for me has always been my nemesis, because I think I don't have enough time, or that I am wasting time when I shouldn't be, during this journey. I was glad to see that others judge themselves by the time spent deciding their next chapter. I have days when I feel that I have too much time on my hands, and there are days when time passes too fast for me to accomplish all my tasks to meet my goals. The funny thing is that they say you only have a short amount of time on this earth, and today will never happen again. Does it matter that you don't have a purpose every day?

The first woman recognized that she judges herself with respect to time. She indicated that she is her hardest critic. She is slowly realizing in the last few years that she never thought about time as a commodity. She said, "Now, because of my personal experience of losing my sister, what am I doing with my time, in order to do things for my nephews, my parents, or for myself? I have gotten closer to my parents because I never thought I would feel that way. I feel guilty about wasting my time because my sister doesn't have any more time on this earth. She was diagnosed, and within 10 months, she was gone. I use time to be productive, whether that is with the job search, going for a walk, going spinning, or reaching out to someone to show I care about how they are doing. Sometimes I feel that it may be too late for me to reach out to people I have worked with in the past. For example, I reached out to someone who reported to me before, to be told that it's the wrong time to connect because her mother just had a car accident. I told her not to worry about me but to go look after her mother. All I have to do is start to network, start to talk about what I am looking for, and start to refine my script, to let others know what my purpose is now. The inability to start, for me, is why I am searching. I feel it is only so that I will not hear the question of what I have been doing for the last year without a job. I can't say that I have travelled the world over the last six months. My *why* becomes harder to explain from being out of work for 3 weeks versus six months. I assume that the person who asks me is judging me, and that I have to justify the time I have taken off. It always goes back to my priorities. My priority is my family and helping them in any way I can right now, and that takes time."

The second woman doesn't have a concern about time as an issue. She expressed that time is money, and that she knows she can ask for money if she really needs it. She was very candid that she is bored with the amount of time she has every day. She admitted that she spends far too much time on Instagram, posting about her passion for gardening. However, she knows that she is connecting with people around the world, who comment on the beauty that she is posting in her pictures. She said, "There is comfort in appreciating the beauty of this world, which you don't get when you are working. There may be a sad person who is cheered up when I post my pictures. There is a woman in Germany that I follow, who knits, and I like her posts every day. There is a guy in England, who takes pictures of his face, and posts every day, and I found out he is an amputee. I know that I am liking it because he calls me friend. I still know that I am spending too much time on Instagram, so I am trying to do less of it. It was helping me because I was doing my gardening, and it was so nice to see that people didn't think I was crazy. I discovered that people liked the time I was spending posting my pictures as a way of giving back to others. I have always been a charitable person by giving back, because I learn more about myself. I want to work again, and I want to work until I am 65 years old. But I don't feel that time is a factor in finding my next job."

The third woman was feeling panicked by the months passing, because of distractions in her life. She didn't want to feel anxious about it because of other priorities in her life. She had weeks when she felt that time was passing too quickly because of the work she committed to, doing renovations on her home. She was astonished at the amount of work she was doing at home, and she wouldn't have been able to work at the same time.

She expressed, "What is my next step? There aren't any opportunities that I am excited to apply for at this time. I have finances to worry about, which I am drawing upon; although God does tell me it is not going to ruin it. My faith is a battle with my fear of time running out in finding the right job. I realize that it is a test of my trust in God. If I really believe He is the ultimate provider, why am I scared of money running out? I want to be earning so that I don't have to draw on all my savings. It's a struggle between what I know in my head and what I believe in my heart. I need to get to a point where my heart agrees with my head for what He is telling me. Faith is believing and trusting in what is currently not seen. He did tell me that He is going to provide for me. I just need to feel calm and not be afraid. I need to tap into His wisdom daily. When the time comes, He will lead me to the right door. I pray, when I apply for jobs, that he will give me a sign to find the right job. So, when I get rejections, I know that it was the wrong door."

All these insights into the common fears of time make me think I am blessed to have the time to chronicle this journey in finding my purpose again. I challenge you to look at your journey as the time spent to better understand yourself, rather than worry about the perceptions of others when they ask you what you are doing with your time. The next chapter will show you how to plan your next steps to making your re-purpose a reality.

Chapter 8: What's the Plan, Stan?

*"In preparing for battle, I have always found that plans are
useless, but planning is indispensable."*
– Dwight D Eisenhower

8

I believe, when you are searching for your purpose or your next job, you need to have a 90-day plan. I had always done quarterly planning when I was leading operations teams, because results allowed me to plan what actions to continue, while stopping the ones that weren't delivering expected results. Now that I am seeking my next purpose, I am using the same approach. It has taken me time to come to that realization, because I forgot the power of goal setting, and I was just settling to find my next job. I started using a 90-day plan when interviewing for my next job, to show hiring managers that I could hit the ground running because I can train myself, given my career success. From my experience, leaders don't get a new hire training plan given them when they start; they are expected to lead others from day one. Well, that requires a plan to ensure that what I focus on daily is going to provide others with the information, guidance, and understanding of how to deliver on key performance indicators (KPIs). I know this is sounding very corporate, but the same applies to any business that you want to start or have started.

The business of re-purposing yourself requires a 90-day plan so that you do things each day to realizing your new purpose. I have taken to writing out my goals and tracking them monthly to see my actions in completing or updating the progress. I think it's easy to get caught up in being busy, but busy-ness doesn't mean that you are developing a business. The way to track progress has always been to set SMART goals: Specific, Measurable, Achievable, Realistic, and Time Sensitive. It's easy to set goals, but it's beneficial to manage them. Managing yourself takes courage so that you can tell yourself what to do every day. I was used to being told what to do during my corporate life, because goals were imposed on me. Now, I must look at myself in the mirror and tell myself to get ONE thing done a day towards meeting my key performance indicators.

I am setting deadlines that are achievable, so that I stop the ME voice who tells me that I am not accomplishing because I am not finding a job. Let's face it, we need income to feel that our lives can be planned out. I know that my life is being planned out by the goals that I am accomplishing, without getting a paycheck to prove it. That's a big step forward for me, and I know it will be for you too.

Finances are always at the forefront for getting your next job. But somehow, earning income must align with your new purpose. Investing in myself may seem ridiculous when I don't have steady income; however, if I let fear rule my thinking, then my ME voice will too. I know that my marketing plan for my re-purpose must be updated so that I can see what I am achieving to replace my paycheck. I know that my paycheck will come once I am acting on my new purpose. I know that my financial problems will resolve themselves once my new purpose is embraced by others who see the value in building our new future together. No one can make a life without others helping them realize their goals, and together, make dreams come true.

Also, I know that by talking to others about my new purpose, I am envisioning the future with a positive attitude, which has always proved to make miracles happen in the past. I am working on building my new purpose by seeking the feedback from others on steps I can take to influence people. I need to find others who agree to support me in creating my dream of running my own theater company.

I bet you didn't see that coming. I have been taking you on the journey of discovering my purpose by trying to fool you into thinking about how to re-purpose yourself, while all along, I have known my purpose but was too afraid to work on it. It's now or never, as they say. I hope you can do your own self-reflection to recognize your passion so that you can use your talents to make your universe a wonderful world for yourself.

I have been helping others achieve goals because I believe in the power of mentoring and coaching others. I know being human is to avoid judging others, because they judge themselves by the actions they take. I believe that we are put on this earth to treat others as you would like to be treated. So, I want to be treated as valuable, because every human life has value. There were days when I had thought that my life didn't matter, as I said while I was telling you about my depression. Now I know that my life is invaluable, because I have witnessed the changes that I have had the privilege to encourage and see in others. My days of directing plays, doing training, and leading teams have shown me that I can model behavior when seeing the potential for success in others. I know how to ask people questions to get them to stop and think about what actions they need to take to realize their goals. I know how to empathize with their struggles so that they can solve their own problems, without giving them solutions. I know that sympathy will only make me feel better rather than teaching them to feel better about themselves. It takes courage to not tell people what to do because you don't want to see them hurting or confused. But the way to help others is to have them speak about their confusion so that they can get clear about what they want to achieve or learn from their own experiences. We all think differently, so it makes sense not to expect others to think like me. I envy those who understand that they think for themselves, because I have spent far too much time worrying about what others think of me.

I guess it has taken me a long time to understand that people don't care about me. I say that with full confidence versus self-pity. I have been thinking poorly of myself because I don't want people to think poorly of me. Wow, what a terrible way of projecting my feelings onto myself, to only be a victim of my own negative thoughts.

As you find what your re-purposed self looks like, take the time to appreciate what purpose you can achieve in this life. For me, it is using my skills and talents to create amazing theatrical and enjoyable learning experiences for myself and others. I have finally realized that I have been placed on this earth to teach others that you can be anything you want if you know how to manage yourself. For a long time, I was managing others but neglected to manage myself. The secret to life is allowing others to see how you manage yourself so that your character is never compromised by the actions of others. I have always loved change because it represented growth; however, I have known that change is uncomfortable. I am now seeing that my resistance to changes I needed to make within myself has been the cause of my *situational* depression.

I know that acting on my marketing plan continues to be the progress reporting that I need to make to myself, to keep up my positive attitude. I have been blaming myself sometimes for not acting on my plan, but now I know that each small step is leading toward my goal of finding my purpose. I have been looking to others to help me find my next job, which is the essence of networking. However, no one can help me find my purpose in life. So, I have been seeking contract positions to allow myself greater opportunities to find employment, given my deep knowledge within the financial services industry. I am sure that as you search for your next purpose, you will have days when you need to know that others are supporting you. I am fortunate to have my theater company, for which I am blessed and grateful to continue to have a community that shares my passion for creating magical productions. I am reminded that my dream of running a theatre company is my true purpose, and that my struggle to re-purpose myself within the business world continues to be my big problem. I know that concentrating my efforts on sharing my thoughts with you gives me peace of mind, because I know that sharing my wishes and needs helps you to think through what truly inspires you every day.

However, let's be clear that wishes and dreams, without acting, will not get you anywhere. You need to act, every day, toward reaching your goals in creating your purpose in life. As you may recall, the previous chapter featured individuals who were acting on their plans but honestly admitted when they didn't some days. It's funny but getting older is supposed to be the time when you set your pace, because you have run several races in the past. We race to achieve career success; we race to have families; and we race to financial planners to ensure that our retirement plans can support us when we aren't racing anymore.

What happens when you feel like you are losing the race? That's when you start to think that you are the victim of your own circumstances. I am creating my future rather than waiting for it be created. I can manifest anything I want by following people I can influence using my positive attitude. I am done making someone else rich. I am rich and deserve to earn the money by following my purpose.

I am grateful during this time of searching within myself. I can reflect why I was placed on this earth. I have wanted to find peace while I continue to search for how to make my passion come true. Do you feel the same way? You are valuable to your family, your spouse, your community, and yourself. That's what I keep telling myself when I get rejections from job postings for which I have applied. I know that my income problems will resolve itself if I focus on pursuing my dream. I know that you have the same thoughts as well, if you have lived your life to please others like I have. If you don't have a plan, you plan to fail. That cliché still rings true for me, because there are days when I feel like I am failing. If truth be told, I don't have a plan anymore because I know that I must take the next step toward realizing my purpose. Planning is more important than having a plan. I am thinking positive thoughts about what I need to do next to operate my theatre company. Right now, I have the talent and the people who can support my vision. The next thing I need are investors willing to back our common people's theatre. Notice that it's *common people's theatre*, because I believe in the power of community to build theatre productions as a means to bond families, friends, and communities together. This world has become so egocentric that there needs to be a place where people can improve and share their skills together. I am sharing my plan so you can see how you can set goals to further your search in realizing your purpose. Remember to track your progress as you move up your goal pyramid (illustrated on page 134), to stay positive in realizing your re-purposed life.

Long-Term Goals

1. Get publicity for success stories in local media

2. Seek community talent

3. Contract semi-professionals to work for 6–12 months

4.Establish annual business goals

Medium-Term Goals

1. Get investors and arts community developing interpersonal skills

2. Apply for government grant proposal to enhance communities

3. Establish corporation for ongoing expense management

4. Use inventory of props, costumes, and sets to build out initial season offering

5. Seek feedback from community groups to determine structure of program offerings

Short-Term Goals

1. Create common people's theatre management team

2. Rent venue for adults and children's acting classes

3. Develop soft skills through acting classes programs

4. Create season for adults with children, in musicals and plays

5. Seek out talent to contract for music and dance classes

6. Cost for catering dinners and liquor licence – dinner theatre evenings as part of season offering

7. Develop marketing plan of training center for corporate team building events

This plan excites me for my future. I know that it may not be easy to be excited about something you are creating by yourself. I can empathise, because I always enjoyed the company environment where the day's agenda was set for me. I am exhilarated by knowing that the agenda I set for myself will lead me to my purpose rather than just getting through my day. This feeling is something that is invaluable when I look at how my life has progressed thus far. This is fun!

For years, I have been the cheerleader in my workplace, claiming that work can be fun by how you approach it. Well, I am here to tell you that the same approach can be done when you are networking to find your re-purposed life. I know that all the experience and expertise that I have gained over the last fifty years will help me to influence others to see my vision of what the theatre business can become.

Let's face it; life isn't all about work. It helps to live your passion because then the work doesn't feel like work. However, you must remember all the other important work that needs to be done to improve your relationships with your spouse, your family, and your children. We were never blessed with children because we found each other when gay couples weren't raising children. It wasn't acceptable based on societal prejudice. Thankfully, we have evolved to appreciate that love is love, and gay couples can raise healthy, happy, and wholesome children. That takes work! Nevertheless, it takes work to have loving and respectful relationships with my husband, my family, my friends, and my network. Life is constantly working for you, or working against you, based on the choices you make. Learn to make choices that will make the work easier and more enjoyable. Wouldn't you want to be cheerful, playful, and enthusiastic when you wake up in the morning, rather than angry, antagonistic, and fearful during the day?

After living half my life (because I plan to live to 100), I realize that each day is precious, because I am blessed to be living a very healthy life. However, I wonder what I will be thinking about my life when I am ready to leave. I don't want to look back with regret, thinking that I never found my purpose, because God has placed me on this earth to serve others. The only way to serve others is to serve yourself first. How can you do your best work if you aren't living your best life? The work that we all do is how we serve others.

Each day, I make choices that will make my re-purposed life come into focus. I have a healthy regime of working out for an hour to energize my batteries. I know that as the years progress, my body needs attention, and I know, when I don't work out, my body is not operating at 100%. Now, each day, I awake feeling like I need to work out. Next, I have a healthy breakfast, including a protein fruit shake to get the nutrients and vitamins that I need in order to be strong and vibrant. I am a firm believer that I will stay healthy by relying on good food and nutrition rather than medicine and supplements. There are days when I take supplements that provide nourishment when my body is functioning at its peak. I want to rely on good habits to keep my body, mind, and spirit focused on being well.

I must admit that I don't know how to relax. I was using television to numb myself into what I considered relaxation. Now, I take moments to breathe and do some meditation to connect with myself again. There are days when I don't meditate, and I feel it. I get anxious and frustrated easily with myself. These are my shame triggers, because I use some nasty language in my thoughts and words. I am not perfect, but there is beauty in being imperfect! Imperfection allows me to want to continue to improve my thoughts and words to build my character as a loving, charming, disciplined, and respectful person.

Finding your joy in what you do, and not in what you intend to do, has always been my mantra. I have beaten myself up too much for not living up to my intentions. I found that positive self-talk can do wonders for creating positive results. When I find myself saying that I should be doing something, I forgive myself for not doing it because of the thoughts that are holding me back. I recommend you practice a self-management technique, called reframing, so that you can look to what you can achieve each day towards achieving your pyramid goals. I have been blessed to be working with individuals who share my passion for working productively and courageously, to create amazing, quality productions in the community theatre group I have created. I know that when the time comes to build the team I need to make my dream a reality, I will have the talent and the resources to draw on, to elevate community spirit needed to promote, produce, and present great shows that will allow me to improve my interpersonal, relationship, and people management skills. I feel the love and respect when working on theatre productions in my facilitation classroom, because I know how to motivate and provide effective feedback.

The lessons I have learned, to provide a safe environment for people to be vulnerable, is one of my greatest gifts, and I know that inspires individuals to learn from me. I know that when I am learning something new, the fear of failure or not being able to master it quickly always slows down my momentum. However, I have learnt that positive affirmations of the progress I am making helps me to build on my confidence rather than focusing on what I haven't done. That is true for all of us. I love to get a positive perspective on what I can do well and continue to work on things that I find challenging. Human kindness and patience are God's greatest gifts to me, when I look back at my accomplishments when I took on challenges. I have taken self-assessment tests, and I have come to realize that I manifest ideas very quickly but lack the patience to implement them at a measured and progressive pace. I tend to want to jump into the deep end without understanding the basics of how to swim. I am taking time to think out my next steps daily, so that I can work toward my pyramid goals by appreciating the efforts needed to accomplish my short, medium, and long-term goals.

I am very proud of the success I have had in my career thus far, and I want to keep up the momentum to create great relationships, achieve great accolades, and manifest great dreams for myself and my husband. I know that bragging about my accomplishments in the past has caused me to feel ashamed of myself now that I am not earning the same income, performing in the same capacity, or living the same life as I had in the past. I think the beauty in living my best life is to be grateful for what I am doing right now. That has taken a long time for me to realize, because I have always compared myself to what others have. I know now that I can only be happy with the gifts that God has given me, without asking why He didn't give me the great mechanical skills my father possessed. I am letting go of the feeling of being unworthy, which started years ago when my father wanted me to succeed in his business. I chose to leave my hometown to explore my own creativity, instincts, and curiosities. I guess me being gay was the underlying fear that I could never be happy living in a small town, because I had always dreamed of being in the big city. Now, I am grateful for having lived my great life full of drama and excitement, to better understand how people communicate and associate, rather than following the path of complacency that I have seen in my fellow family members. I know that my life is worth living, not just enduring, until the end. That is the greatest feeling of self-importance, which no one or nothing can take away from me.

I know that you are probably wondering what you can learn from me as you pursue your new re-purposed life. Here's a great question that someone once asked me: "Who do you go to bed with—your parents or yourself?" I was struggling to be my authentic self as a productive and proud gay man during my acting school days. I had always thought I was fooling everybody by telling others I was going to settle down with my wife and two kids, and live a life in my nice home, with a white picket fence. Well, let me tell you that I am much happier not settling to live up to what I thought was my parent's expectations, and living my life with my wonderful husband for the last 27 years. I feel blessed that I didn't settle but made our own life on our terms. Now that I am over 50, I am proud of the family, the friends, and the life we have made together.

I know that you may feel pressured to settle for anything that you can do that can earn you an income, when you are in career transition. Remember that there will always be ways to earn money, but there is only one way to earn self-respect. Self-respect is when you awake in the morning feeling energized to live that day as if it was your last. So, if this was your last day, how would you feel? Would you be grateful for the love you have experienced? Would you be happy knowing that you have fulfilled your life goals? Would you be content knowing that you are leaving this world a better place than you found it? Would you say to your spouse that you did everything that what was asked of you to make your life together the best it could be?

Let's face it; nobody cares about you more than you care about yourself. Why not answer these questions every day, because that is what people will say about you when you are gone. At least, I hope that is what is said about me, that I lived a healthy, happy, and prosperous life, and that I made my world a better place for the people I inspired, by the example of His love, passion and kindness.

Ultimately, life is what I create, manifest, and commit to achieving. I recently attended the celebration of life for my husband's aunt, who had a long life. In the end, her health declined rapidly, after losing her husband after 54 years of marriage. She was such a loving, caring, kind, and inclusive person, who saw the best in others and always made people feel comfortable and welcomed into her life. She was an amazing example of a nurturing and loyal mother, grandmother, wife, sister, friend, and colleague, who showed how to balance work and life, which is never easy. I know that she re-purposed herself several times during her lifetime, and I am following her example. In my own way, I owe my, and my husband's, life to her—Aunt Dora—who welcomed us into her family with love and kindness. She is my angel now, and I will always be grateful to her for showing me the true value of family.

The next chapter will show how important it is to think that you are winning the race by the pace you keep, not by the hurdles you face.

Chapter 9: Going the Distance When You Think You Can

"I think about myself as like an ocean liner that's been going full speed for a long distance, and the captain pulls the throttle back all the way to 'stop,' but the ship doesn't stop immediately, does it? It has its own momentum and it keeps on going, and I'm very flattered that people are still finding me useful."

– Leonard Nimoy

9

I have been doing a lot of self-reflection as I write my thoughts and feelings during my re-purpose life journey. I know that finding a job is my purpose now in my life, because I need to make an income. However, it doesn't mean that it is a problem that I need to spend all my time thinking about. I am on this journey to learn more about myself and what I want to achieve in the second half of my life. I bet you are thinking the same thing if you have read this far. So, let's take time now to have a serious talk about what Saturdays feel like to you.

Saturdays have always been my days to unplug and recharge. Now I find that as I search for the next steps to be responsible to my re-purpose, I am releasing my guilt about every day feeling like Saturday. While I was in deep depression, I would hate waking up to thinking that I had no responsibilities, and no one was relying on me to show up. I didn't have a purpose for waking up because I was wallowing in my own self-pity, thinking that no one cared if I lived or died. How pathetic is that? I know that I have spoken about the five stages of death when dealing with job loss, but I want to highlight some triggers for you to recognize when you are stuck in the self-pity that can bring on your shame.

From my research, I know that guilt is how you feel about a situation, whereas being ashamed of yourself is attacking your character. For a long time, I was feeling ashamed of myself; I was having my own pity party because I was unemployed. All I was doing was holding myself back because I was ashamed to reach out for help to refocus and reframe my thinking. I remember when my best friend saw that I was in deep depression and was playing Bruce Springsteen's "The Rising," to get me to feel better about myself. As I heard the lyrics and listened to the chorus, I saw my friend dancing and singing along, inciting me to get up and do the same. Unfortunately, I refused to be helped because I was stuck in my self-pity stage, but now I accept the things I cannot change, so these lyrics ring true for me.

> Can't see nothin' in front of me
> Can't see nothin' coming up behind
> I make my way through this darkness
> I can't feel nothing but this chain that binds me
> Lost track of how far I've gone
> How far I've gone, how high I've climbed
> On my back's a sixty pound stone
> On my shoulder a half mile line

That was how I was feeling when I thought I had no purpose anymore. I was feeling weighted down, despite seeing myself shrink as I was losing weight. I had one control over myself, and it was the amount of time I spent working out, how much water I was drinking, and what I was eating. I was holding onto anything that gave me a sense of responsibility. I am now coming up for the *rising*, because I am not allowing myself to indulge in the pity party anymore. I have too much talent and skill to dedicate to the purpose I am creating, and I don't need to live in the past or the future, but for right now. So, I choose to be productive on Saturday and not feel like I need to charge my battery after working all week at a job that isn't fulfilling my spirit. My battery is charged when I use my daily affirmations, seek out new books to read, and learn new things each day to embrace technology, to improve my communication skills. You can live each day like a Saturday, because Saturdays feel like a day to relax. Relaxation is not shutting down but charging up.

I know that by tracking my progress to my goals, I don't feel guilty on Saturday or taking any day of the week for my Saturday. The perspective you gain by seeing how far you've come means that you can unplug from being in constant search mode and charge yourself by being by yourself. It is important to have alone time to think about your next steps in making your re-purposed life a reality. Each day only has 24 hours, but if you take two hours, and call it your Saturday, that is the time you relax and reflect on what you are doing and what you have done during the 120 hours from the previous five days. Also, I am always asking permission to talk about what I need from others as I develop my re-purposed life planning, because I respect that others have their own Saturdays. The expectation now of responding to requests for information provides pressure for you to respond instantly. Well, take time to breathe before responding to others, so that you are ready to use your charged energy to inform rather than be criticized for what you don't know.

I know when my battery needs charging now. It's when I am hearing but not listening to others who care about me. I am blessed to have friends and family who have worried about me during this journey. I have blurted out my intentions without giving them context as to the thoughts and the ideas that I have entertained while planning my re-purpose. My purpose in the first half of my life was to make a living leading other people to conform to corporate rules and principles. The rules are changing in the workplace, and I know that I can make a difference in using my talents to coach other people to lead themselves to defining their own rules of how to work. My philosophy of working the way you want to be means that you work on how you are being, not just on what you are doing.

> *"Eighty percent of success is showing up."*
> – Woody Allen

I have learnt that justifications are lies we tell ourselves, so that we think we look better in the eyes of others when we don't live up to our agreements. My agreement to you in writing this book is to guide you through the experience of making changes in your life, to help you find your re-purpose. I have been detailing some personal experiences, as well as those of others, to help you recognize the stages of death that you experience when dealing with job loss. The reason I am doing this is because I know that you have probably dedicated your life, made sacrifices, and maybe created bad family relations as you focused your time and energy to working and building your career. Well, now is the time to act and create your future with some simple ways to identify your feelings and thoughts as you explore your next steps. Below you will find some personal observations so that you can recognize which stage you are in currently.

Anger – this is the easiest emotional state to identify, because you have a heightened sense of self-importance. I know that when I spoke of my release, it was in anger, because I had been the go-to person for three years. I was in constant demand and was shaping the culture, and I was setting expectations on delivering quality and competence in managing client expectations. I was angry that a re-organization was the reason that my role became redundant. I was mad that I trusted my manager to help me through the changes, and I felt used for my knowledge and let go. I was heartbroken that the five individuals who relied on me for guidance, support, leadership, and security would now be faced with challenges that I no longer could advise. I was bitter and wanted to be part of a tribe, because that was how I was identifying my value as a manager of training who was going to make a difference for all the millennials for which I felt responsible. This stage lasted some time for me because I didn't know how to transfer my energy into making positive changes in my thoughts, to appreciate the time I spent investing in my skills rather than the people who would be missed when I left.

Denial – this is a stage that I was reluctant to face. I transferred my feelings of anger into feelings of resolution that I was going to find my next job quickly because I had great connections within the financial services industry. I joined an association of training and learning professionals to find that my experience and education was lacking in comparison to individuals I was meeting. I was ignorant of the technology and the principles of adult learning, as I had always learnt how to train by my willingness to share my deep financial services and customer service expertise. While I was working, I denied myself the opportunity to educate myself, and now I felt inadequate by chastising myself for years lost, instead of the great knowledge I had gained.

Self-pity – this was a constant nagging that I wasn't good enough when I was attempting to market myself. I was networking and thinking that I would take an opportunity that had an element of training to still be valuable. The more I applied for postings online, the more I was wishing I was still working as the manager of training, because I was responsible for the hiring and onboarding for the client services team. Now I was feeling depressed, and I longed for an ability to have acknowledged the changes that were occurring, rather than living in denial over the last year as the manager of training.

Bargaining – this stage was how I was dealing with the time passing and the feeling of being ashamed of being unemployed at this stage in my life, when I had imagined I would be retiring by 60, but now I was using my retirement savings to stay afloat. I was bargaining with myself as to what and how much energy I should put into finding my next role. I would negotiate with myself each morning as to whether I would ever find my next role and be happy. I was extremely jealous of others who were able to find their next job, because I believed that I was spending more time than others in practicing my interview skills, researching job postings, and applying, without getting responses or rejections. I was bargaining with God when I went to church, asking Him to show me what to do, and I promised I would change myself to meet my next employer's expectations.

Acceptance – I have come to accept that I won't be called back to the workplace that I loved as the manager of training, because that was the past and this is the present. I have accepted that I have lots of skills to learn and can learn one thing well each day. I am proud of the connections I have made, which I never would have had I stayed where I wasn't appreciated anymore. I am looking to the future with optimism and excitement, because miracles are occurring for me. For example, I have discovered the love of writing, which appeals to my creative side. I am living a life of joy when I work with my community theatre company, because I see the potential to fulfill my soul. I know that planning and timing will bring about the future I need for me and my husband.

I am showing up for myself to find a way to earn the money we deserve, to have a life that is rich in love, joy, and prosperity. I know that miracles are happening when I meet new people who can help me define what I need for my next step. I am working to prepare myself for an opportunity to facilitate learning experiences, because that is my purpose. I know how to get people to be vulnerable and feel protected by encouraging them to think differently about their potential. I have tremendous empathy and enthusiasm for people who are willing to work to accomplish their goals. So, I am ready, willing, and able to make my new life in this second act an amazing and awesome journey of discovery of the stamina of the human spirit.

I am learning to be resourceful and rely on myself to achieve my goals. I am learning that discipline and determination are the qualities that no one can take away from me. I am proud that I have taken control of my health by focusing on my eating, my exercise, and my mental well-being. I am confident that my talents are being appreciated and acknowledged, by the compliments I have received from family and friends, and by the positive energy and words that I am expressing. I have improved my organizational skills so that I am ready to confidently speak to others about what I am looking for in my next chapter. I am showing up to be a clear, competent, credible, and compelling leader, who will add value to any organization.

Every morning, before I leave the house, I thank God for giving me the intelligence, the energy, and the aptitude to adapt to the changes I am experiencing. I have a positive perspective that I will be employed so that I can earn money to follow my passion. Let's face it; starting a business takes finances, and I have the plan to do contract work while I follow my pyramid plan in Chapter 8. I know that time isn't against me as I go out and learn to brand myself to achieve amazing things. I know that waiting to be acknowledged is gone, and I need to promote myself. I am not waiting for a promotion anymore because those days are a part of my first act in this life. The second act will be the one when I am on stage, proudly declaring my ups and downs that are shaping my life's story so that I will own my destiny. What is your destiny? What are you the proudest of when speaking with others? What are you going to leave as your legacy? What moments in your life will you look back on and be grateful to have experienced? What way will you know that you made a difference in your life to benefit others? What can you do today to make your tomorrow brighter, smarter, and easier?

By answering these questions, you can start your next chapter of your life to find out how to continue to live your purpose. I know that sounds very existential, but I believe that you are placed on this earth to fulfill God's purpose. I believe that your purpose is to make the world a better place, whatever your world represents. My world, for a long time, was climbing the corporate ladder; but now, my world is to make the lives of others healthier and happier than they are currently. I have been blessed to see some great success occur for others during their search for their next chapter. That inspires me to share some reflections of what that means in understanding your journey.

I interviewed a former member of my networking group, who landed a position using recommended tactics learnt while sharing in our meetings. She had the fortunate circumstance to work with her former manager, who was also searching, after the two had been released after working together for some time. She was able to build her network from zero, and to engage former colleagues and fellow job searchers to seek the same role as IT project coordinator. She tried and tried to find similar roles, because she felt comfortable following her heart to find another coordinator role within the telecom sector. She was happy to be using her current skills, and she chose to focus her energies on how to brand and market herself, knowing that she was going to find another role within the industry. Her self-esteem and self-confidence were essential for her to build her skills in using LinkedIn, and to meet with key individuals to find hidden opportunities.

She told me that she wanted to focus her energies on how to brand herself and not feel the need to reinvent herself. I admired her tenacity because she was eager to learn all she could while she was using her company-sponsored transition resources. She indicated that she was concerned that she was going to be viewed as obsolete, but she decided to make her network work for her. She was in contact with individuals that were in the telecom industry, who could introduce her to people with whom she could speak about hidden opportunities, to continue using skills that she had acquired for over twenty years.

Luckily, she had stayed in contact with her former manager, who offered her a position in the company with which he had landed a position after they had departed together. She confided in me that she felt very fortunate that the timing of the role being offered was perfect for her. She had an opportunity to enjoy her sabbatical without feeling the financial pressure to settle for a role in which she would not continue to use her customer service skills to her advantage. She had consulted with her financial planner, and budgeted her expenses, to avoid feeling anxious while she used her newly found networking skills. She confirmed that she was very careful not to bring old habits into her new company, as they warned her that she would not have access to the same resources that she had in her former company. She highlighted that she has affiliated herself with a younger employee, to learn from her how to be efficient in using the company tools and resources so that she could easily adapt to the new working environment. She believes that she must stay current and work to present herself as vibrant and young so that she can acclimate herself with her new team.

She is grateful for the support she received from her network contacts, and personally thanked them when she landed her role. She recommended that you take time to express gratitude for the introductions and connections you make during your search, as she recognizes the importance of remaining connected and branded while she adapts to the culture and expectations of the workplace. She confided that she was in a cocoon for far too long, because she was inwardly focused on her previous employer, and now appreciates that her world has expanded dramatically. She expressed that her adaptability has improved, because she knows that she will be making mistakes and learning from them to keep learning and growing in her new role.

I was impressed with how she was sharing her experience so that I could include a success story within this book to inspire and motivate you to find your re-purpose opportunity. I have learnt the value of kindness to others and to oneself. I have been unkind to myself during this process of transformation to find how I am going to use my talents and skills in my future. I have been complimented for my ability to empathize and summarize peoples' success stories as they prepare for interviews. I have been honored to share my expertise from interviewing hundreds of people during my twenty years in managing teams. Lastly, I have come to recognize my ability to coach and mentor others, to refine their thoughts and feelings to gain a positive perspective when dealing with the ups and downs of hiring processes. I consider myself very fortunate to have received kindness and to be kind to others when meeting individuals and seeking their help in finding my re-purpose. I recommend you think about ways that you can be kind to others as you go through your self-discovery. The way

I express my kindness is to always compliment individuals with a smile, to let them feel better about themselves. I have loved seeing the smiles on people's faces when paying them a compliment. I also know that kindness is contagious, and I am making a difference in brightening someone's day.

I know that asking others for help can make you feel uncomfortable or desperate, but everyone can use help in understanding how to make their goals come true. I believe in a give-get contract, and always ask what I can do for someone when they offer to help me. I know that asking for help for me was easy because I am always willing to help others whenever I can. I have come to appreciate that everyone is willing to help when they can; it just may not come as fast as I want. I have learnt the value of patience and perspective when networking because everyone has their own schedule and time for when they can give to you.

I have been using my network to help me understand how to be the right person at the right time. I know that my planning is coming together to bring me the right role in which I can use my talents and skills to make a better life for my husband and myself. I must admit it is hard sometimes not earning an income but still building my skills. I am ready and able to take on my next role as a facilitator, speaker, coach, and teacher, as I continue to live my re-purpose.

All this time, I have been feeling like I am running out of time. Wow, why is it, when we are younger, we feel the days pass like hours, and now days pass like years. I worry that I will not have the time to do everything I want to accomplish now that I know my re-purpose. I know that I am taking on many roles and responsibilities to make my dreams come true. I also know that multi-tasking is a fallacy. The definition of multitasking originally came from running the concurrent performance of several jobs concurrently. Human beings aren't computers, so my focus is to do one thing well a day, so that I can manage the multiple projects that I will accomplish over the coming year. I am pacing myself every day, to stay energized and available to opportunities to improve my aptitude and my skills, to meet the agreements I have made to myself and others. I have been documenting my progress so that I am able to see the completion of my goals. I am always running to my next opportunity, but I know that I need to walk sometimes as well. For example, I am appreciating that I am learning to research, review, and renew my skills to be free to express myself with confidence and competence. I have always been the person to *fake it until I make it*. Well, my *faking it* days are over, because I am developing my skills that will highlight my talents to communicate, negotiate, and educate others on how to live their best lives and earn the income they deserve, practicing servant leadership. It is my honor to serve you as you explore your talents while realizing your re-purposed life skills. The next chapter will reveal how all this comes together to make you put your re-purposed life into action.

Chapter 10: What's Your Legacy, and Do Others Care About It?

"My legacy is that I stayed on course... from the beginning to the end, because I believed in something inside of me."
– Tina Turner

10

You have now come to the point in the book where you need to put thoughts and actions into making your re-purposed life happen. You have been reading about my reflections and my self-discovery journey that hopefully has inspired you to avoid the pitfalls of depression, shame, and disappointment in yourself, by doing some work to take stock of your talents and skills. I know the value of journaling my thoughts and feelings daily to provide myself with positive confirmation of the progress I am making. I recommend you do the same. I know, to form new habits, it takes repeating them for 21 days. I am a believer in writing in my journal every morning to get perspective on what I can accomplish that day. Also, I know it allows me time to reflect on what miracles occurred the following day. Some have said that writing in a journal at the end of the day allows your mind to rest more easily. You capture your thoughts by writing them down, to avoid reflective thinking, causing you to have a restless night. It is entirely up to you how you wish to document your thoughts—just do it!

If you recall, the first chapter of my book was about *knowing thyself*. I know more about myself from the reflections I have captured while writing this book. I am not suggesting that you write a book to decide how to re-purpose your life. However, I ask that you take time to answer the following questions, to understand how you think and feel, and what you want for your life going forward. Here are the questions that I want you to answer as you get to know yourself better:

What kind of music inspires me?

What kind of people do I like to associate myself with?

What was the most productive day I had in my career?

What are the qualities of the best boss I ever had?

What qualities do people notice most about me?

How much money do I need to make to be happy?

By answering these questions, you will start to see what motivates you to be your best. You will wake up and know what satisfaction you are seeking in being productive as you build your life on your terms rather than someone else's. I know that typical question, of what you would do if you weren't afraid, would make sense to be included, but you will be afraid to start this journey, because it will be different from what you have always known. That's okay, because it will take time to adjust to this new way of thinking about how you use your skills to benefit your new re-purpose. I am afraid every day, thinking that I still have a lot of skills to learn, based on my re-purposed life, to make my life goal come true while training and facilitating to pay the bills. That's what life is all about: making the best of the hand that is dealt you, while you find out how to use your passion to make money.

Staying the course means that you are inspiring your children to follow their dreams, because you are now doing the same. I believe that children listen to what you say but learn from what you do. They learn about integrity, honesty, determination, trust, and commitment from the actions you are taking to make your life fulfilling now that you are taking control of your destiny. I have not been blessed with children but have been fortunate to be included in my nieces' and nephews' lives, who tell me that my passion and dedication to following my dreams has inspired them to live their own. I am grateful for my sisters and brothers-in-law, who have always included my husband and me whenever possible, to influence their children to be responsible, intelligent, and inquisitive, and to build healthy and happy relationships. That has always been my priority, to shape and influence them through our actions and beliefs.

I am not expecting to be famous, but I am expecting to be loved by my family until the day I die. I am shocked when I hear of other families where the siblings don't associate because of disputes over assets that are divided up when parents pass on. I made the choice to stay involved with family members because my parents taught me the value of family. Do you want the same for your children?

One of the greatest lessons I have learned is the ability to laugh at myself and to enjoy the highs and lows of making the best of my life. I know that change isn't easy now that you are finding your joy in your new re-purposed life. Well, that is what you are here to do; to find joy within yourself so that you can give it to others. You will have challenges that you will face as you learn new skills to explore the talents you want to show the world. However, you can have fun learning them by seeking out groups and individuals who are experts in the field in which you want to be involved. I know that my association with the Institute for Performance and Learning has allowed me to upgrade my skills in building training sessions that are interactive, engaging, and entertaining, because I want to use my acting, communication, and relationship talents in my re-purposed life. I am grateful that others are willing to share their joy of training so that I can learn from them what I should focus on, and how to market myself. That is one of the lessons that you will need to learn:

the value of branding to grow your skills. You will be able to find the joy within yourself to share with others as you continue to build relationships to strengthen your re-purpose.

Remember that the concentration you need, in order to stay focused each day toward meeting your goals, will make the journey more enjoyable by doing the following: branding yourself on social media, tracking your progress in your journal or pyramid goal setting plan, measuring your success through the number of opportunities that are now appearing as you market your re-purposed life, and managing your happiness by earning the compensation you deserve.

There will be days when you will wonder why you are doing this. *Why don't I just get a job and be happy?* Well, it is up to you to find your joy and happiness, so remember that it is a decision that you make every day. You need to know that there will be ups and downs as you stretch yourself to find what you need to develop to realize your re-purposed life. It may be that you need to do online courses to improve your skills, so that will take time and money. Remember, you are investing in yourself, so any opportunity to learn will benefit you in the long run. Choose fun rather than fear, when deciding to explore your talents, since they are gifts that only you can present to the world. Don't be afraid of what others think, because they are more afraid of developing themselves than you could ever be afraid of yourself.

Staying the course means that you are true to yourself during the second part of your life. I have always thought that second acts are far better than first acts, because all the setups for the laughs have already been established. Notice that I said *laughs*, because you are now comfortable to face the ups and downs of repurposing yourself, if you have followed along with my lessons. I know that you will be going back to chapters so that you can recall the wisdom that I was providing you, to manage the emotional ups and downs during the transformation that you are experiencing, in identifying the skills you need to easily re-purpose yourself. The skills for me to enhance are my branding skills, using social media to attract individuals to build my coaching business, communication skills as a professional speaker, building relationship management skills via networking platforms, and facilitation skills to encourage the use of acting skills to develop family dynamics and help children connect with parents and adults. What are your skills that need enhancing?

All the world is a stage, so don't wait until you miss your cue to enter your next play. The plays that you are planning to make will never happen unless you face the fear of failure. I know that I am facing that fear every day, and by marketing myself as the authority on job loss, I have faced my fear of not feeling worthy. Also, I have put myself in front of others as the person they can trust, by having the courage to talk about my depression and isolation. We are all hurting, and sharing my story is a way for me to realize my re-purposed life of helping others achieve their goals in realizing their re-purpose.

If you follow your heart, God will show you the talents you have been given. I know that some of you may not believe in God, but you can believe in yourself. You have the power to make anything you want happen, if you put your heart into it. Passion stimulates others when you speak, so you need to find every opportunity to speak about what you are passionate about. I have spoken to you about feeling like nothing while I was in the depth of depression. I had equated my life to not being worthy of love because I was thinking I was too old to get a job. I had tried many times to shake those thoughts but felt isolated and trapped in my own negativity. I had to see that being something is better than being nothing, and that for me to accept myself as being worthy of love and respect, it had to come from inside myself. No amount of money, no position in an organization, and no praise for being a team player is going to validate that I am good enough. I am better than good—I am great! I decide every moment how to manage my day, because I am not allowing someone or something else decide that for me.

You can see that I am blowing my own horn so that the world can hear and see that I am a winner and not a loser. Please remember that God doesn't make mistakes—people do! So, don't let your mistakes define who you are by not learning from them. There are ways to promote your talents that I never had when I was growing up. Today's kids know how to be the *rock star* by doing videos on YouTube, posting podcasts, building websites, and posting on Instagram. So, why can't you? I am embracing the ability to promote my brand and grab the attention of my audience so that I can be the *rock star* I always wanted to be. I am accepting the compliments and cheers from my Facebook friends as autographs, because my voice is needed during times of change, rather than trying to change my voice to suit others' needs. My voice is confident and credible because of my years of experience. I have the expertise to create entertaining and enjoyable learning moments so that YOU can work the way you want to.

What do you want to be when you grow up?

About the Author

Alex J. Bodnar was born in Woodstock, Ontario, Canada. He moved to Toronto, Ontario to attend York University, and discovered his passion for the theatre. He pursued his passion upon completing the Music Theatre Program at Sheridan College. He worked as a professional actor for eight years. Then he worked his way up the corporate ladder, starting in the mailroom by educating and leading others, using his first-class customer service techniques. He worked for many years within the financial service sector, leading award-winning client service teams, while creating onboarding programs inspiring young individuals to aspire to professional and personal achievements. He continues to live his passion by directing and performing in community theatre, while sharing his life over the last 27 years with his loving husband, Sean, and their two cats, Millie and Stanley.

He offers insightful and energizing coaching sessions, using his skills in co-active coaching to help you realize your potential in exceeding your business, professional, and personal goals. He can introduce you to his program by providing a complimentary assessment of your skills and talents, to plan your re-purposed life.

He is a professional speaker and will gladly speak to you and your company about the challenges of career transition, health and wellness, and resilience.

You can contact him directly by email at AlexJ@turning50today.com.

Visit his website to learn more about his Re-Purpose Yourself, six-month coaching program, at www.turning50today.com.